The Excel Advanced User's Guide

The Excel Advanced User's Guide

Richard Loggins

HAYDEN BOOKS
A Division of Howard W. Sams & Company
4300 West 62nd Street
Indianapolis, Indiana 46268 USA

For Hyon C. "Billy" Brown,
who taught me (among other things):

"Hana, dool, set, net.
Tasut, yausut, ilgope, yaudul."

International Standard Book Number: 0-672-46626-0
Library of Congress Catalog Card Number: 87-60109

Acquisitions Editor: BILL GROUT
Manuscript Editor: SHARON COGDILL
Cover Design: JIM BERNARD
Cover Photo: CELESTE DESIGN
Indexer: SUSAN HOLBERT
Compositor: TYPESETTING SERVICE CORP., PROVIDENCE, RI
Produced by: EDITORIAL SERVICES OF NEW ENGLAND INC.
Production Coordinator: TRAUTE M. MARSHALL

Printed in the United States of America

Contents

Preface

Five years ago, any book that didn't tell you how to turn on your computer might have been considered an "advanced" book. That, of course, was during the time when people were still trying to figure out what a spreadsheet was and, more important, just what they were supposed to do with this electronic equivalent of pencil and paper.

But as people began to recognize the value of these electronic marvels and started using them in their business and personal lives, spreadsheets underwent major changes to keep pace with the demands made by what quickly became known as the *sophisticated* or *power* user.

More and more features were added to spreadsheets until these once simple products became so complicated that it was hard to keep up with the many options available and relatively easy to become "lost in the forest." As users quickly learned, sophistication brings complexity.

Today, few — if any — spreadsheets can rival Excel's sophistication. But unfortunately, sophistication (now often called *functionality*) is worthless without understanding.

In this book I've tried to strike a balance between the basic information that's required of every user and the topics that let you take full advantage of the power available to you with Excel.

ix

I've tried to distill all of the crucial information you need to make effective use of Excel, to zero in on the vital information you won't find in any other book, without delving into extremely complex applications of somewhat dubious value.

This book uses simple English to explain many of Excel's features, including:

- Excel's concept of integration
- ways that macros can be used for something more than automating menu functions
- the capability Excel has for designing forms
- exotic uses such as personalized form letters
- the use of more than one database per worksheet simultaneously

By studying (and more important, understanding) the information presented in the following pages, you'll be able to achieve results you never thought were possible. And as always, if you get hung up on a particular item or want the worksheets, macros, and applications on disk so you don't have to type them in, all you need do is drop a line to

Richard Loggins
P.O. Box 39
Sugar Run, PA 18846.

Introduction

Either you've already purchased Excel and are looking for a book that will help you capitalize on Excel's true power and flexibility, or you're considering buying Excel and are trying to decide if it's worth the investment. In either case, the single most important question now in your mind is whether or not this book will help you. The answer, perhaps surprisingly, is a *qualified* yes.

If you own Excel and don't know it's possible to have more than one active database on a single worksheet, if you believe Excel is three applications in one package like many other software packages, if you don't understand how to develop sophisticated integrated applications, then this is the book you're looking for.

If you're considering buying Excel, this book will explain what Excel is capable of and how you can apply the program to your situation. It isn't intended to compare or evaluate the major integrated software packages available, and may make an occasional comparison to specific features on other products.

Before diving into the maze of worksheets, functions, and macros, you should be aware of a few key points that will make it easier for you to use Excel effectively.

First, Excel is *not* a clone of 1-2-3® or any other spreadsheet. Excel is a sophisticated tool that

- lets you define how data should be manipulated
- permits multiple perspectives of the same data, and
- applies the true meaning of the word *integration*.

Thus, instead of being three different applications (four if you count macros) in one package, Excel is a single tool that lets you bring individual units of information together into a whole.

Once you quit trying to apply the "three-in-one" concept of integration to Excel and begin viewing it as a single application that is capable of supporting an astounding number of perspectives, you'll be surprised what you can accomplish in a relatively short time.

Just as specific quantities of flour, sugar, butter, and vanilla can be combined to make delectable delights or atrocious concoctions, so it is with Excel's formulas, functions, and macros: properly used, they will ease your most difficult tasks, automate repetitive and time-consuming procedures, and improve your productivity.

This book is unlike the vast majority of books that promise much and deliver little. It does not use the same terminology, methods, and procedures used in other books to explain the sophisticated and seemingly endless number of options available to you when you're using Excel. Neither does it profess to be a book only for beginners or advanced users. Such philosophies make too many assumptions and usually fail to help you attain a true level of competence.

This book has one purpose: to teach you how you can use Excel effectively and efficiently, in the shortest possible time, and with the least amount of frustration. It will dispel many of the myths surrounding Excel — like Excel's being limited to a single active database per worksheet. It will correct the dangerous procedures given in the *Excel User's Guide* — like placing your criteria area *above* your database area during data extraction.

Further, you'll discover how to overcome the largest single deficiency of most Excel users: failure to take advantage of Excel's most useful feature — true integration. Integration lets you maintain your documents separately (like income, expenses, and forecasts), while simultaneously integrating the key elements of each into a cohesive report. Integration provides the important facts essential to decision making without bogging you down in details.

In the pages that follow, you'll learn specific tasks, like how to

- implement more than one database area on a single worksheet
- establish multiple active criteria areas for each database, so you can take full advantage of Excel's data manipulation capabilities
- use tables and arrays effectively to increase the speed and flexibility of your applications
- explore Excel's forms design capabilities to create meaningful reports
- design and implement fully integrated applications that will increase your productivity dramatically.

Further, you'll have access to complete, predefined applications that you can use immediately or modify to suit your needs.

Audience

The Excel Advanced User's Guide is intended for anyone who understands the basic operational procedures of Excel and the Macintosh and wants to become proficient using Excel in a business, professional, or personal environment. Moreover, it is specifically aimed at the individual who wants to use Excel to increase productivity without pursuing a career in data processing or computer programming.

All of the material is presented in a simple, straightforward manner, making it easy to understand each topic and how you can implement the methods and procedures in your applications.

Organization

Each chapter in this book examines a different aspect of Excel. Hands-on examples and suggested exercises are used to solve typical problems that every businessperson must contend with.

The part you're reading now, Chapter 1, provides you with the overall organization of the book, what you can expect to learn, and a brief synopsis of the subjects covered in each chapter.

Chapter 2 examines the importance of design and documentation. You'll learn the correct procedures and methods that will help make your integrated applications successful.

Chapter 3 presents the keys to effective integration when using Excel. It emphasizes the importance of addressing modes and their use, the identification of common mistakes, and the role of named references in making your applications more effective.

Chapter 4 shows you how fixed tables can expand the versatility of your applications, make seemingly difficult tasks easy, and give meaning to the term *what if*. You'll discover how arrays can be incorporated into your applications, making the task of data manipulation even easier.

In Chapter 5, you'll be surprised to learn that Excel doesn't actually have a database. You'll learn how to create multiple active criteria areas and multiple active database areas on a single worksheet, how several database areas can share the same criteria area simultaneously, and how to use computed criteria.

Chapter 6 introduces the basic concepts, procedures, and commands used to create command macros. By writing a macro that will create a Loan Information worksheet, you'll come to understand the advantages of command macros and how they can be used to ease the construction of worksheets.

In Chapter 7, you'll begin creating a major integrated application that is controlled entirely by one macro sheet. You'll learn how to use macros for data entry and verification, transform simple worksheets into functional menus, replace repetitive procedures with a single *subroutine*, and much more — including working with several worksheets simultaneously.

Chapter 8 completes the application started in Chapter 6, and shows you how to determine the quantity of data on a worksheet, organize it into usable form, extract and summarize specific data, and create dynamic reports without touching a key!

In Chapter 9, you'll learn how to use Excel for designing multiple- and single-column forms that look as good as printed invoices, reports, and so on. You'll examine the procedures for manipulating text that can be incorporated into your macros to print personalized form letters, interoffice memos, and other documents.

Using This Book

The material in this book is presented in a simple, straightforward manner. Carefully designed, "hands-on" examples are integrated with the appropriate amount of theory to provide you with a *true* level of competence using Excel.

Each chapter in this book contains examples that illustrate the requirements, results, and implementation of the commands and procedures involved. Wherever possible, the examples are brief and intentionally simple (that's simple, not useless) to reduce your typing and to prevent the example from overshadowing the commands, procedures, and methods. By actually performing the procedures given with each example, you'll gain the in-depth knowledge required to use Excel effectively, efficiently, and consistently.

Above all, *take your time!* The high degree of functionality in Excel must be understood to be useful.

CHAPTER

Design and Documentation

Design and documentation are the cornerstones of any application, regardless of its size or complexity. A properly designed and documented application requires less time to implement, reduces the size of your worksheets and macro sheets, executes much faster, is easier to use, and is easier to modify to accommodate future requirements.

This chapter teaches you how to design and document your applications correctly, so that they will perform as expected. Although design and documentation are intertwined, they are presented separately to provide you with a clearer picture of their individual importance and to let you focus your attention on one subject at a time.

Designing Integrated Applications

The design of any application can be divided into four major elements:

- Identifying the major objectives of your application
- Specifying which worksheets, macros, and reports will be used

7

• Implementing and actually developing your application
• Verifying that the completed application meets the original objectives and works properly

To place the importance of each step in proper perspective, assume that you've been given the task of developing an inventory system for a bicycle manufacturing company. (The methods and procedures apply to any application and are not limited to this particular one.)

Identifying Objectives

The first step in identifying your objectives is to gather information about the present system (assuming there is one) or the proposed system.

A good way to start is by speaking with everyone involved, from managers and supervisors to secretaries and data entry personnel, making notes of what each person does and doesn't like about the current methods and procedures. Ask what each person thinks could be done to improve the way things are done.

Obtain a copy of every form and report that's used, making a note of who uses it, why, and what information it lacks. Compare these to see how much duplication exists (you'll be surprised) from form to form and report to report. Find out if forms or reports can be combined, making sure you know why or why not.

Depending on the size and scope of the operation, you might want to develop and circulate a questionnaire to supplement your conversations. A questionnaire, however, should never replace personal contact. People respond much better to people than to questionnaires.

If you decide to use a questionnaire, the following two questions may unearth key problem areas that need to be addressed.

1. Does anyone contact you regularly for specific information? If so, who contacts you and what information do they want?
2. What information do you need that you are not currently getting?

The results of your conversations, questionnaires, forms, and reports will probably be a mountain of information that must be analyzed to identify the most important objectives of your application. The major objectives — and they should be limited to no more than ten — should be listed together on a separate sheet of paper. (Major objectives include items that are needed and that are essential to performing the job; minor objectives are nice but not necessary.) In our bicycle manufacturing company, such a list of major objectives might finally look like this:

1. Automatically notifies user when inventory items are at or below reorder points

2. Compiles parts lists for specific bicycles

3. Automatically updates price lists based on the cost of raw materials

4. Reduces inventory levels based on sales orders

5. Automatically computes sales commissions

6. Increases inventory levels as purchase orders are filled

Minor objectives you feel are significant or that are closely related to the major objectives should be listed together on another sheet for possible inclusion in your application.

Specifying Worksheets and Macros

The key to specifying which worksheets and macros you need is to explore the available alternatives and decide which alternative will best suit your needs. Every application, regardless of its size, has more than one acceptable solution, although many are not necessarily the best.

By examining your list of major objectives, you should be able to identify the items that are directly or indirectly related. In the example used here, three of the six objectives are directly related to the inventory (item 1, checking inventory against reorder points; item4, reducing inventory based on sales; item 6, increasing inventory based on purchase orders). The remaining three items are indirectly related to the inventory. Thus, the key worksheet in this application is an inventory worksheet (called Raw Material in this example).

Once the key worksheet has been identified, you can explore alternatives and decide which path to take. For example, consider the first objective, which is to automate the process of notifying the user when inventory items are at or below reorder points.

One alternative is to create a separate worksheet with external references to the Raw Material worksheet that displays an asterisk when any item is at or below the reorder point. The other alternative is to include the same function on the Raw Material worksheet.

Creating a separate worksheet named Stock Status reduces the quantity of information appearing on the monitor or in a report, making locating and analyzing specific items much easier. On the other hand, incorporating the stock status information into the Raw Material worksheet reduces the total number of worksheets in the application by placing all the data on a single worksheet. Thus, deciding whether you need a Stock Status worksheet is a matter of deciding how much information you want to see on the Raw Material worksheet and deciding how many worksheets you want.

Compiling a parts list and automatically updating price lists (objectives two and three) can be solved in several different ways.

First, you could create two separate worksheets: one containing the parts listing, which includes the component costs, and a second one, using external references to the Parts List worksheet which summarizes the total cost of each product. This would link the Price List worksheet *through* the Parts List worksheet to the cost figures contained in the Inventory worksheet. Changing the cost of a particular item on the Inventory worksheet would immediately update both the Parts List and Price List worksheets, since they are linked to the Inventory worksheet.

Other alternatives are to combine the information on the Price List and Parts List worksheets into a single worksheet, or to link both the Parts and Price List worksheets directly to the Inventory worksheet. Again, which alternative is best depends upon your needs.

Objectives four and six, reducing inventory based on sales and increasing inventory based on purchases, are best handled by a combination of worksheets and macros for several reasons.

First, in any transaction specific data will be transferred between several worksheets: the Sales Order, Purchase Order, and Raw Material worksheets. This is a potential source of errors, since the Sales Order and Purchase Order worksheets may be similar in appearance and content.

Next, there is less possibility of an error if a macro is used to find the correct part number and either add to or subtract from the current inventory level. A macro, operating correctly, will perform the same operation every time without fail, and it never tires of repetitive, tedious tasks.

Finally, it is essential the inventory is adjusted without duplicating previous transactions — easily overcome by using a macro to keep track of transactions.

A Sales Order worksheet can be used to maintain the basic information concerning each sale, such as customer, item, price, but a macro would be used to update the inventory and customer files by adjusting inventory levels and customer purchase records.

A virtually identical approach could be used to accommodate purchase orders, substituting vendor information in place of customer information.

The final objective, computation of sales commissions, again could be either a single worksheet containing all of the necessary information or a combination of worksheets. If you're maintaining a significant amount of information about your salespeople that will be used for more than just commissions, or if you prefer to keep certain information (like commission rates and schedules) confidential, a combination of worksheets should be used. Otherwise, a single worksheet is easier to manage.

Once you have decided on the worksheets and macros you'll use in your application, the next step is to create a diagram that shows their relationships to each other, similar to the one in Figure 2.1.

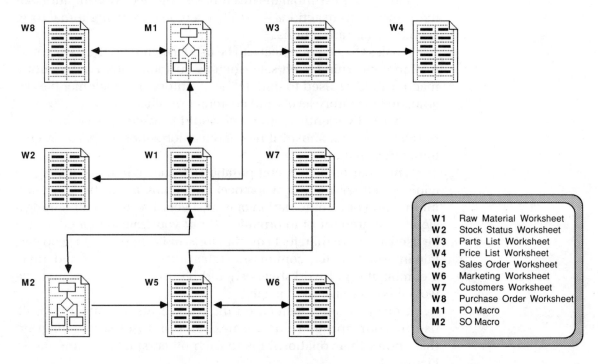

Figure 2.1 Application diagram identifying worksheets and macros
and their relationships

The application diagram in Figure 2.1 not only identifies the worksheets and macros, but uses interconnecting lines to show their relationships. Additionally, by assigning a code to each one (such as W1 for Worksheet 1), you can incorporate a brief description of each worksheet.

In any integrated application, one worksheet is the cornerstone of the entire application; it is located by arranging (and rearranging) your diagram until no two lines cross. Once identified, this worksheet should be developed first, since all other worksheets will access the data it contains.

In the application diagrammed in Figure 2.1, the Raw Material worksheet (labeled W1) is the key worksheet. Its information is accessed or manipulated either directly or indirectly by all of the other macros and worksheets in the application.

Even though you might be tempted to choose the Sales Orders worksheet as the key worksheet, it is disqualified by the type of information it will contain. Any sales order will refer to a product, which immediately tells you that certain information must be obtained from the Raw Material worksheet. A more prominent indication is the SO macro, since macros are normally used to transfer data between two worksheets. The SO macro cannot obtain any information about the product if the Raw Material worksheet does not exist.

Implementing Your Application

Implementing your application is primarily limited to creating the actual application and verifying its operation. This includes flow charts (if you're using macros), worksheet construction, form and report design, and above all — *testing*.

When implementing your application, always create your worksheets first, then your macros. If you create your worksheets first, you'll know exactly what cells contain the data your macros will access and what display formatting will be used. Ultimately, this sequence will reduce the number of modifications you'll have to make; further, it will help you identify the source of an error, especially when you're working with macros, since you'll know that each worksheet has been tested and operates correctly.

During the creation of worksheets, make use of the special formatting options offered by Excel, such as bold and italic displays, cell borders, gridlines and row/column headings, and even custom numeric formats. These items can change dull, drab worksheets into works of art that are easier both to use and to look at.

Never sacrifice an appealing display to save a couple of cells. Excel supports over 4,000,000 (that's million) cells, and you won't save any money by not using them.

After you've created your worksheets, enter data into each cell to make sure they operate correctly. Also, be sure to look at what happens when you enter invalid data and to test for extreme conditions. For example, if sales are normally less than $9,000.00, try entering a number like $999,000.00 or even a negative number.

Test macros in a similar manner by entering both expected and unexpected types of data. For example, if a macro asks for a Yes/No response and accepts either "Y" or "N," try entering some other letter. Better yet, don't make *any* entry and click OK.

Verifying Operation

Once you're satisfied with the results of your operation, go back and check your list of objectives and verify that your application does everything on your list.

Most important, remember that your application is not complete until the proper documentation has been prepared and the system has been used extensively in actual situations for at least 60 days. (Many people recommend six months, which is fine for extremely large or complex operations or in instances where the entire operation will depend upon your application.)

During the time your program is in actual use, make sure the old system is maintained. By comparing the results of the old and new systems, you'll be able to verify the integrity of your application as well as have an "insurance policy" should one system fail.

Documentation

Two types of documentation, end user and program documentation, should be an integral part of your applications. End user documentation explains the operational procedures of your application and tells the user what the application does, how to use it, and the results that it will provide. Program documentation explains the formulas, functions, and macros from a programming point of view to ease any modifications.

Program Documentation

Program documentation is developed the same time as the application, and it is revised into final form when your application is complete. Depending on the size and complexity of your application, the documentation may include the following.

- **Data Diagrams**   A data diagram, a pictorial representation similar to the one shown in Figure 2.2, shows each worksheet and macro used in the application, as well as their relationships.

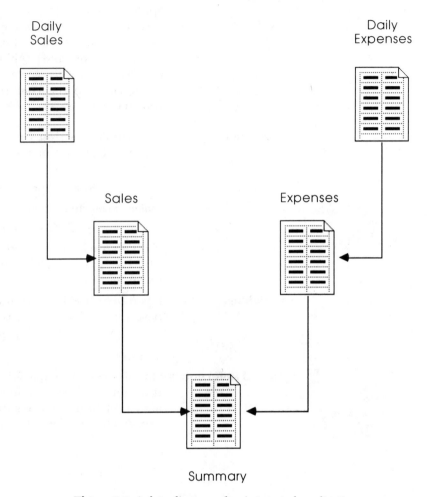

Figure 2.2 A data diagram of an integrated application

- **Flow Charts**

  A flow chart, a diagram showing each function your application performs, is used as a guide to help ensure that the logic of your application is correct. It expresses operations in English terms instead of computer commands. (Although specific symbols are used to depict certain operations, you can create flow charts from rectangles or ovals, as shown in Figure 2.3.)

- **Formulas**

  All formulas used in your application should be expressed in both mathematical and algorithmic terms. For example,

  $$\text{Profit} = \text{Income} - \text{Expenses}$$

  makes it easy to understand the formula

  $$\$D\$1 = \$B\$1 - \$C\$1$$

  if it's expressed as an algorithm and contains $\$D\$1 = \text{Profit}$, $\$B\$1 = \text{Income}$, and $\$C\$1 = \text{Expenses}$.

- **Variables**

  If you use variables in your applications, provide a description of each, such as

  $$\text{EXP} = \text{Expense, PRO} = \text{Profit,}$$

  and so on.

- **Named References**

  One of Excel's most powerful options is its ability to use named references. Although named references are easier to use, make sure your documentation explains the purpose of each one.

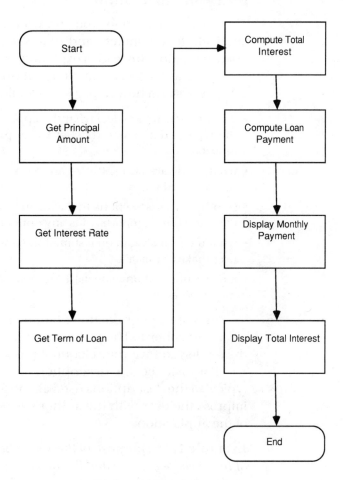

Figure 2.3 Sample flow chart

User Documentation

The documentation for the end user is usually developed after the application is complete and differs significantly from the program documentation. Instead of explaining such things as the macros and the formulas, end user documentation emphasizes what the application does and how to use it. It should contain and explain:

- general information, like what the application does, how it is organized, the type of data entered, what the application will return in terms of reports,
- what hardware and software are required for operation, especially any nonstandard items
- step-by-step instructions that explain how to start the application, enter data, and obtain reports, plus any options available to the user
- what the user should do if something does not operate correctly or if the user makes a mistake
- a description of any special terminology used in the application or its documentation

In writing your documentation, make sure the descriptions are clear and concise. The purpose of your documentation is to inform the reader, so save your eloquent passages for your autobiography.

For instance, the description of an application in Example 1 is typical of the descriptions used all too frequently in a vain attempt to impress the user with the author's expertise and the sophistication of the application.

Example 1: *The purpose of this worksheet is to provide the end result of the revenues generated by the various marketing efforts after taking into account the impact of the funds distributed to maintain operation during the first six-month period of the last calendar year.*

Although this description may sound impressive, it uses too many words and imparts very little information. Contrast it with the description given in Example 2.

Example 2: *This worksheet shows the profit made during the first six months of 1986.*

Naturally, larger or more sophisticated applications require more documentation than smaller applications.

If you aren't enthusiastic about writing your own documentation, and assuming your application warrants it, you can retain the services of a technical writer at a cost ranging from $10.00 to $75.00 per hour, at a negotiated rate for the entire task, or even for an initial fee plus a percentage (generally 10% to 20%) if the application will be distributed. The better the writer, the higher the cost (usually).

In selecting a technical writer, you should always ask for:

- a resume or similar document describing the writer's background and experience
- references from the writer's previous clients
- an estimate of when you can expect completed documentation
- the type of word processing equipment available to the writer
- a sample of the writer's previous works
- a written agreement

Make sure you read the writer's samples (often called *clips* or *tear sheets*). If you can't understand what the writer is saying — regardless of academic credits — or if you simply don't like that writer's particular style, by all means look for another writer.

Summary

In this chapter, you examined the four keys required to correctly design and implement integrated applications — identification, specification, implementation, and verification. You saw the alternatives available to help you decide which worksheets and macros you'll need in your applications. You examined the essential ingredients required for proper documentation of your applications, so that modifications to your applications will be easy to make. You learned the requirements for end user documentation and how to evaluate a technical writer if you decide one is needed.

CHAPTER

3

The Key to Integration

The key to using Excel's concept of integration effectively is to understand addressing modes, named references, and their effects. Once you understand these features, you'll be able to simplify your applications without sacrificing power, flexibility, or speed, and you'll reduce the size of your applications.

In this chapter, you'll gain an in-depth understanding of Excel's addressing modes and named references, including how to correctly apply them in your applications.

Addressing Modes

Although addressing modes are covered in the *Excel User's Guide*, their importance is not sufficiently stressed, and they are not discussed in the context of integration. And since integration is the most useful aspect of Excel, it is absolutely necessary that you understand:

- what addressing is
- what the different types of addressing are
- how to implement them, and
- what the most common ramifications of using addressing are.

21

Addressing modes are used to identify a particular location on a worksheet, much the same as an address on a letter identifies a particular location. In Excel, four primary addressing modes are used: *internal, external, absolute,* and *relative addressing.* Internal and external addressing are used to identify a worksheet; absolute and relative addressing identify a particular cell or a range of cells on the worksheet.

Absolute vs. Relative Addressing

Absolute addressing specifies a fixed, unchanging location, and is indicated by the presence of the dollar symbols in the address, while relative addressing specifies a cell based on its relative distance from the cell containing the address, and omits the dollar symbols.

So if cell C3 contained the formula

$$= \$A\$1 + \$A\$2$$

the addressing would be absolute, since both cell addresses contain two dollar symbols. The result of this formula would be to add the number found in cell A1 to the number found in cell A2, then display the total in cell C3. If the formula in cell C3 would be copied or moved to cell D3, the formula would still add the contents of cells A1 and A2.

Relative addressing specifies a particular row and column on a worksheet based upon their relative distance from another cell on the same or another worksheet. A relative address *does not* contain any dollar symbols. So if the same formula would be converted to relative addressing, it would appear in C3 as

$$= A1 + A2$$

(note the absence of dollar symbols).

Further, if the formula would be moved or copied to cell D3 — which is one row to the right — the formula would be changed to

$$= B1 + B2$$

to maintain the same relative distance from the cell that contains the formula. The formula does not change if it is moved or copied when absolute addressing is used. That the formula itself changes in relative addressing is the primary difference between the two addressing modes.

Internal vs. External

Both absolute and relative addressing can be internal or external, depending on the worksheet they reference. If a formula references cells on its own worksheet, then the address is internal. If the formula references cells on a worksheet other than the one containing the formula, then the formula is external and incorporates the name of the worksheet.

For example, if you were using a worksheet named Worksheet1 and entered the formula

$$= \text{Worksheet2!\$A\$1} + \text{Worksheet2!\$A\$2}$$

into cell C3, the numbers in cells A1 and A2 on Worksheet 2 would be totaled and placed into cell C3 on Worksheet1. Thus, an external address references cells that are external to the worksheet that contains the formula.

For an internal address, the worksheet name is usually omitted from the formula, although you can include it if you want.

To tell the difference between the two types, examine the worksheet name that is included with the address. For example, the worksheet shown in Figure 3.1 contains four formulas:

1. an internal absolute address in cell B2,
2. an external absolute address in cell B3,
3. an internal relative address in C2, and
4. an external relative address in cell C3.

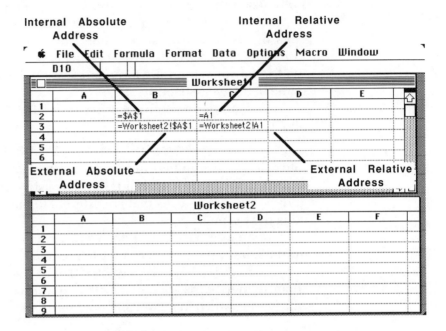

Figure 3.1 The four basic addressing modes

Notice that the external addresses in cells B3 and C3 include the name of a worksheet, Worksheet2, which is separated from the cell address by an exclamation mark (called a *delimiter*). The internal addresses in cells B2 and C2 do not contain the name of a worksheet.

Even though you can include worksheet names in every address — both internal and external — without any detrimental effects, you'll find it is more convenient to omit the worksheet name for all internal references. Not only does this save typing, it makes it easier to tell whether an address is internal or external.

For example, look at Figure 3.2. Suppose cell A1 on Worksheet1 contains the number 999, which represents the cash receipts for the day. And suppose that cell A1 on Worksheet2 contains 444, representing the expenses for the day. Using the formulas from Figure 3.1, the external references in cells B3 and C3 will show 999, and the internal references in cells B2 and C2 will show 444.

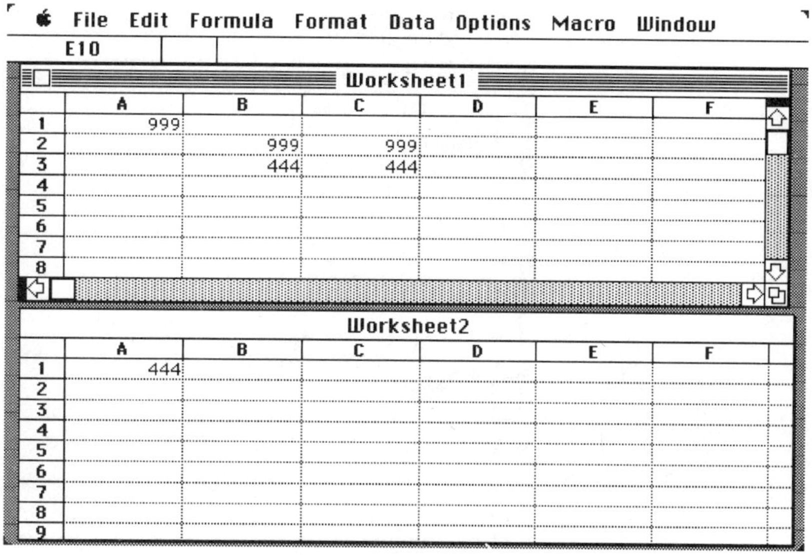

Figure 3.2 Using the four addressing modes to add receipts and expenses

Numbers on a worksheet can be misleading or even meaningless unless appropriate labels are included to identify them. If labels were added to each of the worksheets in Figure 3.2, the numbers would provide meaningful information that would be easy to interpret.

To add the labels shown in Figure 3.3, select cell A1, choose the Insert option of the Edit menu and insert one row and one column.

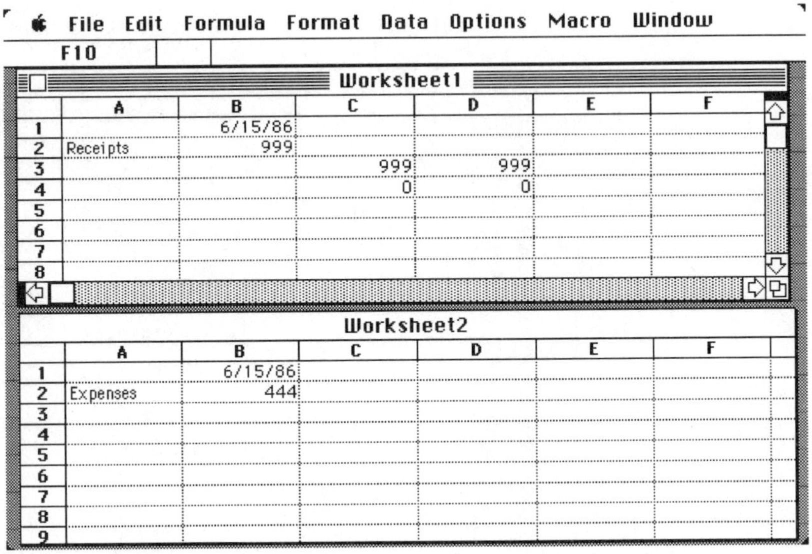

Figure 3.3 Worksheets after insertion of meaningful labels

After the insertion is made and the cells on both worksheets have been moved down and to the right one cell, add the labels "6/15/86" and "Receipts" (on Worksheet1) or "Expenses" (on Worksheet2) to identify the numbers now occupying cells B2 on both worksheets. Your worksheets should agree with what is shown in Figure 3.3.

Notice the effect that this simple insertion has had. The formulas in cells C3 and D3 on Worksheet1 still refer to the proper location and show the number **999**, while the formulas in cells C4 and D4 indicate a value of zero, all due to the different types of addressing used.

If these two worksheets were part of a sophisticated application, a minor change — even to accommodate labels — in any worksheet could invalidate the data on every worksheet in the application.

If you're wondering why the formula in cell D3 still shows the value 999, since it also contains a relative address, the answer is simple: the data in cell B2 is still in the same position *relative* to the location of cell D3. Thus, a cell containing a relative address will give incorrect results only if the *relative position* of the two cells is changed.

This example makes it easy to understand the differences made by the different types of addressing on a single reference to a single cell. It does not, however, illustrate the role addressing plays in formulas and functions.

Consider the integrated application shown in Figure 3.4, which consists of five worksheets: Daily Sales, Daily Expenses, Sales, Expenses, and Summary.

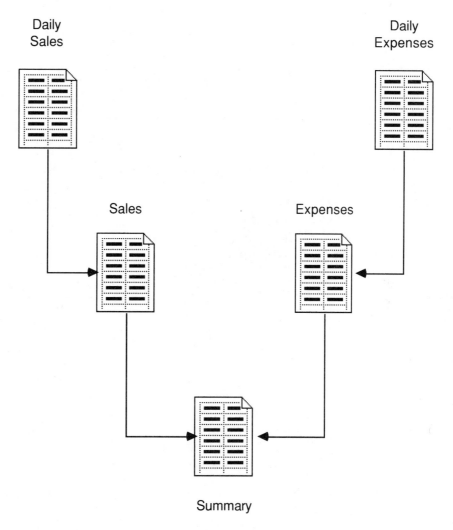

Figure 3.4 Application integrating five worksheets

Two of the worksheets, Sales and Expenses, contain weekly summaries of the daily sales and expenses. These weekly summaries are further summarized and placed on the Summary worksheet so that they will be easy to compare.

Creating the three worksheets shown in Figure 3.5 and entering the information shown will help you understand how various addressing techniques can be used in an integrated environment.

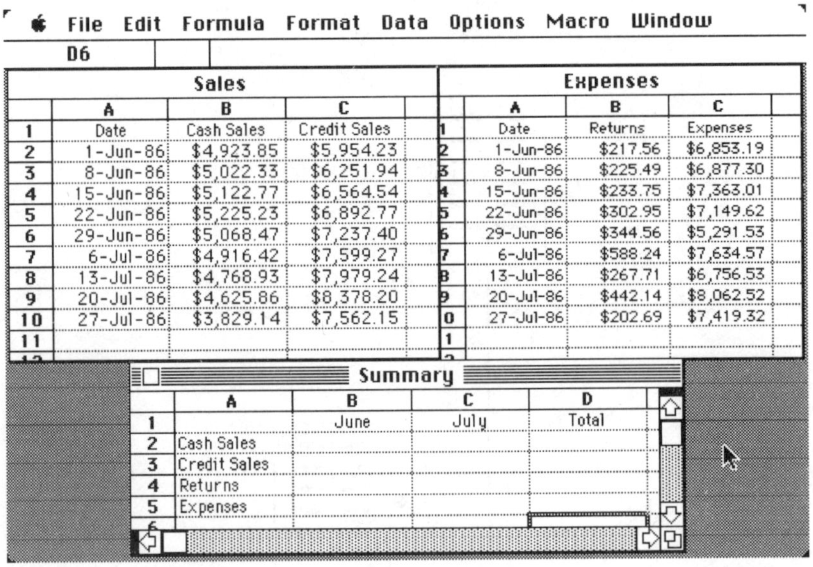

Figure 3.5 Sales, Expenses, and Summary worksheets

The first addressing technique used is perhaps the most common: a separate area on the Sales worksheet is established to summarize the sales data, and this summary information will in turn be accessed by formulas on the Summary worksheet.

Create this area by entering the labels *Cash Sales* and *Credit Sales* in cells F2 and G2, and *June* and *July* in E3 and E4, as shown in Figure 3.6.

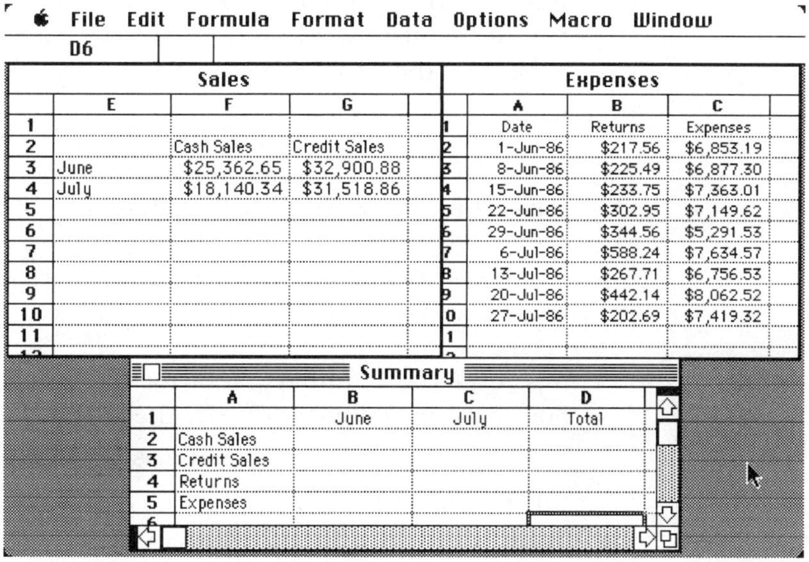

Figure 3.6 Summary areas in Sales, Expenses, and Summary worksheets

Next, total the cash and credit sales and place them in cells F3 through G4 by using the **SUM** function in conjunction with the appropriate cell range.

As you enter the following formulas into the cells indicated, notice that relative addresses are used for the cash sales figures, absolute addresses for the credit sales.

Cell	Formula
F3	=SUM(B2:B6)
F4	=SUM(B7:B10)
G3	=SUM($C$2:$C$6)
G4	=SUM($C$7:$B$10)

While both addressing methods provide the desired results, if the absolute addresses used in cells G3 and G4 are moved or copied, they will still refer to the correct cell ranges. But if the formulas containing relative addresses (F3 and F4) are moved or copied, they will *not* access the correct figures. Try this by selecting F3 and temporarily inserting a cell.

When you do this, the formulas that were previously in cells F3 and F4 no longer contain their original addresses, and change to reflect their new positions, resulting in the incorrect figures being displayed.

If you delete the cell you just inserted, the addresses again change to indicate their original addresses, and the figures are correct.

After the summary area has been established, activate the Summary worksheet and enter the formula

$$= Sales!\$F\$3$$

into cell B2 and

$$= Sales!\$F\$4$$

into cell C2. The external references link the data in cells F3 and F4 on the Sales worksheet to cells B2 and C2 on the Summary worksheet.

In a similar manner, link the credit sales figures by entering

$$= Sales!G3$$

into cell B3 and

$$Sales!G4$$

into cell B4 of the Summary worksheet.

Next, obtain the total cash sales figure by entering a formula composed of internal relative references,

$$= B2 + C2$$

into cell D2 of the Summary worksheet.

Finally, total all credit sales with a formula composed of external absolute references,

$$= Sales!\$G\$3 + Sales!\$G\$4$$

by entering it into cell D3 on the Summary worksheet.

This exercise demonstrates the different ways each of the four basic addressing modes can be used. Internal addressing was used in the summary area of the Sales worksheet, using both relative and absolute addressing; external addressing was used to link the data on the Sales worksheet to the Summary worksheet.

Simply knowing the correct syntax for the basic addressing modes is almost useless unless you know *why* and *when* to use them. Unfortunately, no set of definitive rules can dictate which addressing method to use in a given situation.

Two general guidelines, however, may help you decide which addressing method to use:

1. Absolute addressing is best suited to areas of a worksheet that will not change, such as fixed tables, cells containing predefined variables, and criteria areas.

2. Relative addressing should be used if you expect cells to be moved or copied frequently, either individually or as a group, or to replicate formulas and data to other parts of a worksheet.

For example, consider the three worksheets you've been working with. What would the effect be on the entire application if the Expenses worksheet were combined with the Sales worksheet, as shown in Figure 3.7?

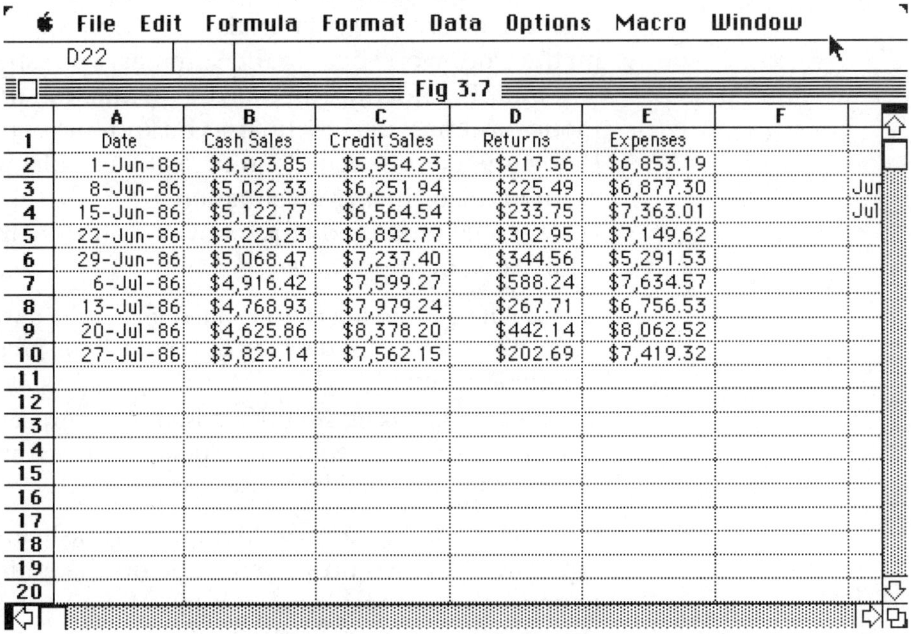

	A	B	C	D	E	F
1	Date	Cash Sales	Credit Sales	Returns	Expenses	
2	1-Jun-86	$4,923.85	$5,954.23	$217.56	$6,853.19	
3	8-Jun-86	$5,022.33	$6,251.94	$225.49	$6,877.30	
4	15-Jun-86	$5,122.77	$6,564.54	$233.75	$7,363.01	
5	22-Jun-86	$5,225.23	$6,892.77	$302.95	$7,149.62	
6	29-Jun-86	$5,068.47	$7,237.40	$344.56	$5,291.53	
7	6-Jul-86	$4,916.42	$7,599.27	$588.24	$7,634.57	
8	13-Jul-86	$4,768.93	$7,979.24	$267.71	$6,756.53	
9	20-Jul-86	$4,625.86	$8,378.20	$442.14	$8,062.52	
10	27-Jul-86	$3,829.14	$7,562.15	$202.69	$7,419.32	

Figure 3.7 Combined Sales and Expenses worksheet

First, additional columns would have to be inserted between columns C and D to accommodate the new information, requiring the formulas in cells F3, F4, G3, and G4 to be changed on the Sales worksheet.

Next, massive changes to the formulas on the Summary worksheet would have to be made. The formulas in cells B4 through D5 refer to a nonexistent worksheet, since the Expenses worksheet has been eliminated; the formulas in B2 through D3 do not refer to the correct locations on the Sales worksheet.

The implications of such a massive change are easy to see, but even minor changes can significantly affect your applications.

For instance, when the August, September, and October figures are added to the worksheets, all formulas in the summary area of the Sales worksheet will have to be changed to ensure that the figures from the additional months are included in the totals.

Named References

There are addressing techniques that can be used to prevent changes on one worksheet from having a major impact throughout your application. These are known as *named references*, and their capabilities extend far beyond what you'll find in the *Excel User's Guide* or most tutorial books.

A named reference is nothing more than a label you create and assign to a cell or cell range. Properly used, named references will, among other things, let you

- modify your worksheets without having to change every formula
- establish multiple active database areas
- manipulate entire cell ranges with a single function
- ease the task of tracing formulas from one worksheet to another

Activate the Expenses worksheet, select cells B2 through B6, and use the Define Name option of the Formula menu to define the name *JuneRet* as an absolute named reference, as shown in Figure 3.8.

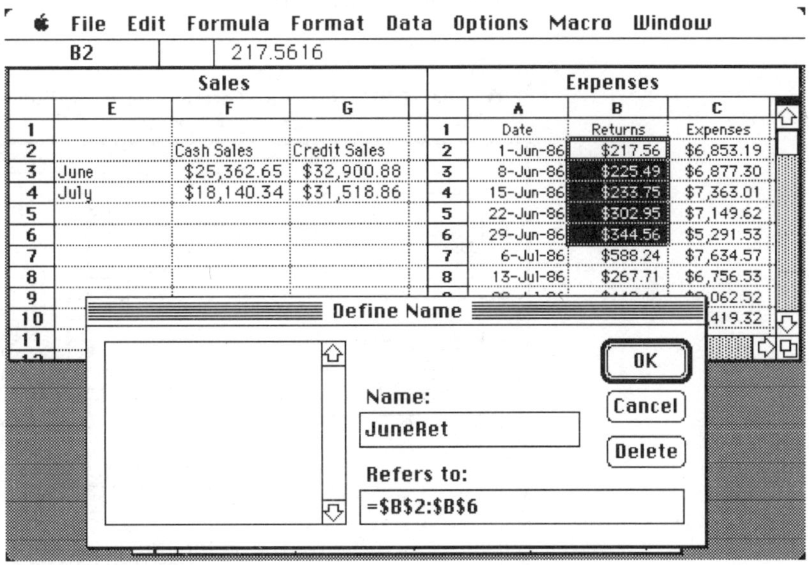

Figure 3.8 Defining *JuneRet* as an absolute named reference

Once defined, the name *JuneRet* can be used to reference the data in cells B2 through B6, since Excel will obtain the definition of *JuneRet* as soon as the name is encountered during calculation.

Further, it is easier to associate the return figures for June with the name *JuneRet* than with the formula

$B$2:$B$6.

To use the name, activate the Summary worksheet, select cell B4, and enter the formula

= SUM(Expenses!JuneRet)

When this formula is entered, the total return figures for June are linked to the Summary worksheet, just as if you had used absolute cell references.

Now, if the June return figures are moved or altered, you won't have to make changes to the formulas on every worksheet in the application. When a change is required, you need only to change the definition of the named reference on the Expenses worksheet, and your application will once again be correct.

The same method can also be used to total the returns for July by activating the Expenses worksheet and defining the name *JulyRet*, as shown in Figure 3.9.

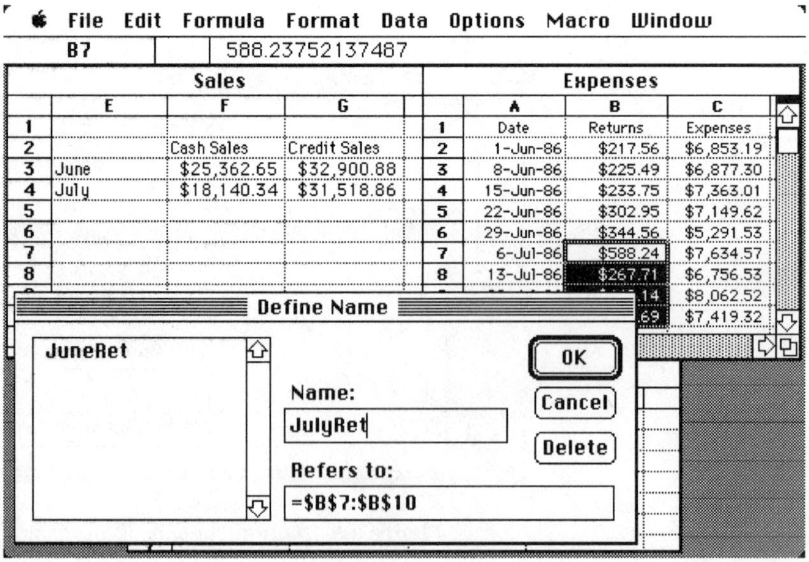

Figure 3.9 Defining *JulyRet* as an absolute named reference

After the name has been defined, activate the Summary worksheet and enter the formula

= SUM(Expenses!JulyRet)

into cell C4. This formula will link the July return figures to the Summary worksheet. Expenses!JulyRet can then be incorporated into another formula (consisting of only one function and two named references), which will total both the June and July returns.

To total the June and July return figures, select cell D4 on the Summary worksheet and enter the formula shown below.

= SUM(Expenses!JuneRet,Expenses!JulyRet)

This variation of the SUM function uses two named external references separated only by a comma. Using two named external references is much simpler than using two separate functions, each containing external addresses.

Using the SUM command in this manner — to total more than one cell range — not only reduces the possibility of typographical errors, it is also easier to understand, as shown in Figure 3.10.

Although this variation of the SUM function — using two named external references — is shown in the Excel User's Guide, people often fail to take advantage of it. As an advanced user, make effective use of your tools!

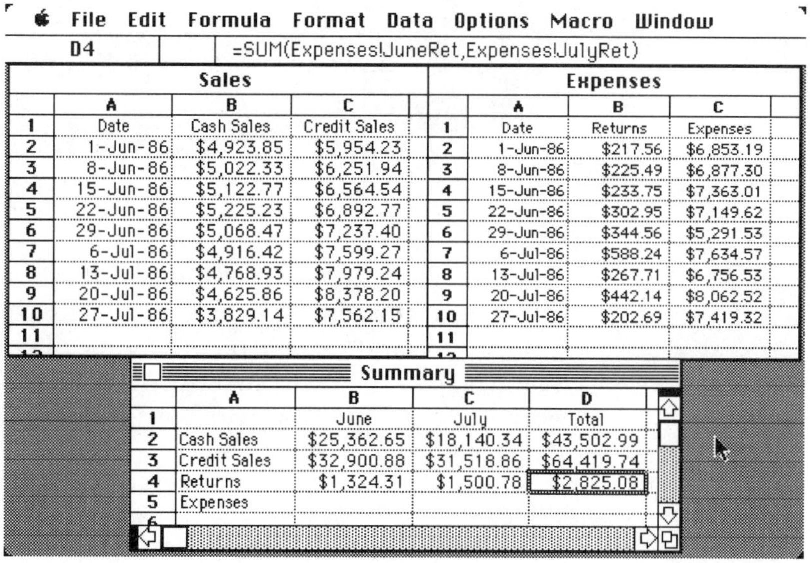

Figure 3.10 Using named external references to summing multiple ranges

Compound Definitions

The last three forms of named references that you will use in this chapter are called *compound definitions* since they combine two separate items — named references or functions — into a single definition, further expanding the flexibility of named references.

Activate the Expenses worksheet and define the name *JuneEx* to refer to cell range $C$2:$C$6. This definition will be used in another named reference to total the expenses for June.

After defining *JuneEx* on the Expenses worksheet, activate the Summary worksheet and make the definition shown in Figure 3.11.

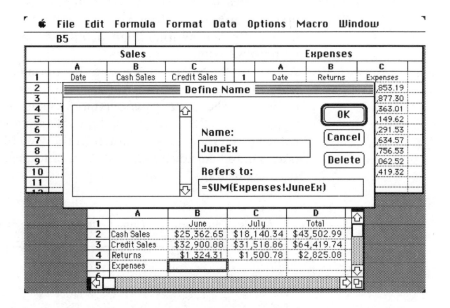

Figure 3.11 Compound definition

Notice that the same name, *JuneEx*, appears on two different worksheets, and that each definition is different. By using the same name on different worksheets, you can easily keep track of the links you establish between worksheets, since you need to trace only a single name.

When you enter (or paste) this name into cell B5 on the Summary worksheet, the figures in cells C2 through C6 of the Expenses worksheet are totaled and placed into cell B5, as shown in Figure 3.12.

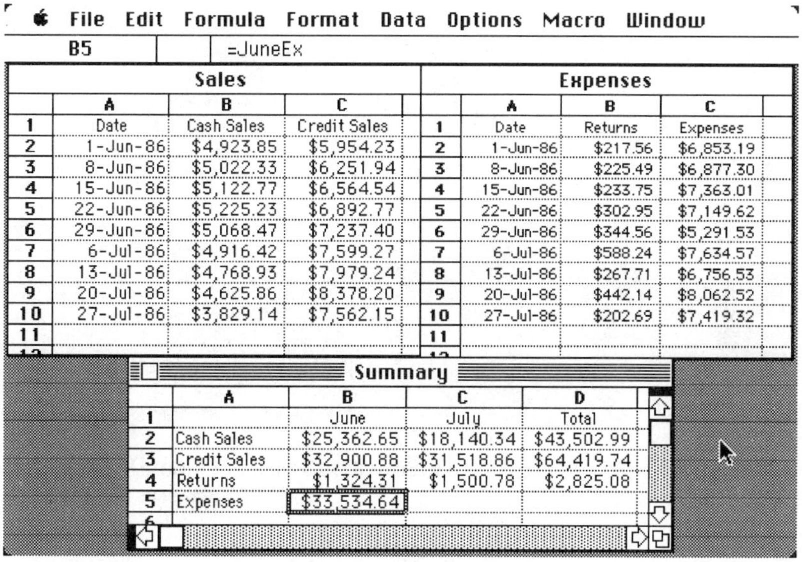

Figure 3.12 Using compound definition for June expenses on Summary worksheet

There is a still better method for using a compound definition: place the compound definition on the Expenses worksheet instead of the Summary worksheet, as shown in Figure 3.13.

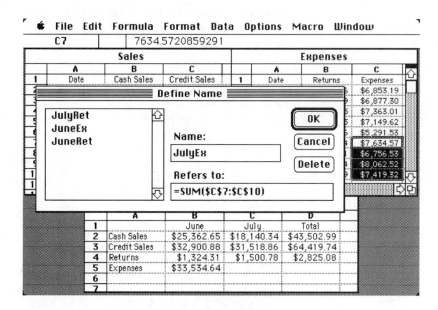

Figure 3.13 Using compound definition for July expenses on Expenses worksheet

The same name, *JulyEx*, can then be defined on the Summary worksheet and be used the same way the JuneEx definition was used. The primary advantage of this method is that the formula is easier to read. This makes tracing named definitions from worksheet to worksheet still easier.

Finally, the definitions for obtaining the total expenses show that using the same name on two different worksheets can be helpful. It can also be confusing if you let it get out of hand by using the same name too many times.

To show you how easy it is for named references to become confusing, activate the Expenses worksheet. Define the name *Expenses* as the sum of column B by inserting the formula

= SUM($B:$B)

into the Refers To box. This will sum an entire column, and any additional entries in the column will be included automatically in the total. Further, any non-numeric entries (like the column title) will be ignored during calculation, assuming that additional columns are not inserted or deleted.

Next, activate the Summary worksheet, define the name *Expenses* as

= Expenses!Expenses

and paste the name into cell D5 of the Summary worksheet.

Now, if you trace the definition of Expenses on the Summary worksheet, you'll find that Expenses is Expenses!Expenses is Expenses. Using the same names for different purposes leaves you ample opportunity to change accidentally one of the named definitions instead of column headings or vice versa.

Avoiding Danger

Every example in this chapter has used absolute addresses for all named definitions. And if you have given thought to using relative references for greater flexibility, remember this: *under no circumstances should you ever define a name as a relative address*. Doing so will only guarantee that your worksheets will contain erroneous data, and you'll spend hours pulling your hair out trying to figure out what happened.

When a named reference uses relative addressing, the relative address always refers to the currently selected cell. So if you define *Zap* as the relative address C3 and then select cell A1, you'll find that the definition for Zap has been altered to refer to cell A1.

Next, never use the name *Database* or *Criteria* as the definition for a cell or cell range. Every time you access either the Set Database or Set Criteria options of Excel's Data menu, Excel automatically creates these names and assigns them to the currently selected cell range, thus eliminating any other definitions of the names *Database* and *Criteria*.

Summary

In this chapter, you examined the four different modes of addressing (internal, external, relative, and absolute) and the effects of using each in an integrated environment. You learned the two general guidelines for deciding whether absolute or relative addressing should be used and how each can be successfully incorporated into your applications to expand their functionality.

You used named references to reduce the possibility of errors, ease the manipulation of data, and make it easier to trace formulas through several worksheets.

You learned the advantages of using compound formulas and named references that incorporate external references and functions to minimize the effects of any changes. You learned that math operations on entire columns automatically exclude any non-numeric entries.

You'll use this knowledge through the rest of this book as building blocks for more sophisticated operations and applications.

CHAPTER

Fixed Tables
and Arrays

Excel supports two types of powerful data manipulation functions which are known as fixed tables and arrays. Fixed tables and arrays are not related to the Table option of the Data menu. Where the Table option of the Data menu produces a series of results based on a single formula, a fixed table returns a value that corresponds to a single entry within a given cell range, such as a commission rate associated with a sales figure.

Arrays, on the other hand, are composed of a specific cell range that can be manipulated by special commands or used as a fixed table. For example, you can multiply the corresponding values in two columns simultaneously with only one formula.

Both fixed tables and arrays can make the manipulation of similar data structures — such as the various items in an inventory — easier and faster, since you can use single commands and functions to operate on an entire cell range instead of formulas and commands for each individual operation.

In this chapter you'll create four of the worksheets that appear in the bicycle manufacturing company application diagram shown in Figure 2.1 of Chapter 2, to create an inventory, produce a parts list and a price list, and automatically compute sales commissions based on predetermined sales volume.

41

The first worksheet, named Raw Material and labeled W1 in the diagram, contains the basic data that will be used and manipulated by the Stock Status, Parts List, and Price List worksheets (labeled W2, W3, and W4, respectively), through the use of fixed tables.

You'll use arrays to expand the functionality of your applications through the use of the special commands that are associated with arrays, and you'll learn how arrays can be used simultaneously as fixed tables. As an advanced user, you'll be able to incorporate these methods into virtually every type of application that requires access and manipulation of data. These data, which must share a similar form to be useful in fixed tables and arrays, can range from stocks and bonds to inventory, real estate, fixed assets, and so on.

Raw Material Worksheet

Since no formulas were used in the Raw Material worksheet, create it by simply entering the information shown in Figure 4.1.

	A	B	C	D	E	F
1	Part No.	Description	Cost	In Stock	RO Point	
2	100-00	Frame	$28.67	40	21	
3	100-01	Handlebars	$14.35	71	18	
4	100-02	Hardware Package	$3.18	85	31	
5	100-03	Pedal, Left	$0.43	55	22	
6	100-04	Pedal, Right	$0.43	16	22	
7	100-05	Rim, Front	$2.87	18	28	
8	100-06	Rim, Rear	$3.12	58	33	
9	100-07	Reflector, Red	$0.02	59	15	
10	100-08	Tire, Standard	$1.53	23	21	
11	100-09	Seat	$2.96	54	29	
12	200-01	Fender, Front	$3.05	85	40	
13	200-02	Fender, Rear	$3.69	83	40	
14	300-00	Light	$4.35	21	24	
15	300-01	Mirror	$2.02	22	21	
16	300-02	Reflector, Amber	$0.03	25	15	
17	300-03	Reflector, White	$0.03	76	15	
18	300-04	Tire, Off Road	$2.11	28	21	
19						
20						

Figure 4.1 Raw Material worksheet

After you've done that, you must define six named references that are used by other worksheets to access the data on the RawMatl worksheet.

To create the first name, select cells A2 through E18, then use the Define Name option of the Formula menu to assign the name *RawMatl* to cells $A$2:$E$18.

Next, select columns A through E, choose the Create Names option of the Formula menu, then click the Top Row option to establish the labels shown in row one as the names for the columns. Choose the Define Name option of the Formula menu and make sure that your named references agree with those shown below.

Name	Refers to:
RawMatl	$A$2:$E$18
Part_No.	$A:$A
Description	$B:$B
Cost	$C:$C
In_Stock	$D:$D
RO_Point	$E:$E

Since, by definition, the name RawMatl refers to the entire worksheet, RawMat1 can be used as a fixed table to locate and extract any of the data on the worksheet. The names you assigned to each column will be used to compute and locate the data in each column.

Thus, any cell range on any worksheet can be referenced simultaneously with multiple names as well as by its address. This gives you greater flexibility in accessing your data.

After defining the names, save this worksheet with the name Raw Material before constructing the remaining worksheets. Otherwise, the external references you enter in subsequent worksheets won't refer to the correct worksheet, and they will generate an error value.

Stock Status Worksheet

The Stock Status worksheet uses several of Excel's table-oriented functions (LOOKUP, MATCH, CHOOSE) to monitor continuously all of the items on the Raw Material worksheet. Whenever the quantity of a specific part falls to a level equal to or below its reorder point, the Stock Status worksheet will display three asterisks.

Create the Stock Status worksheet by copying the information that appears in cells A1 through A18 on the Raw Material worksheet to cells A1 through A18 on the Stock Status worksheet. After copying the data, enter into the first row the information shown in Figure 4.2.

	A	B	C	D	E	F
1	Part No.	Description	On Order	Status		
2	100-00					
3	100-01					
4	100-02					
5	100-03					
6	100-04					
7	100-05					
8	100-06					
9	100-07					
10	100-08					
11	100-09					
12	200-01					
13	200-02					
14	300-00					
15	300-01					
16	300-02					
17	300-03					
18	300-04					
19						
20						

Figure 4.2 Stock Status worksheet

To obtain the descriptions for each of the part numbers, use one of Excel's table-oriented functions, called LOOKUP, to find the part number that appears in column A of the Stock Status worksheet and return the description shown in column B of the Raw Material worksheet.

The LOOKUP command has three parameters associated with it; the *lookup value, compare vector,* and the *result vector*. The first parameter, the lookup value, specifies the item you're looking for — in this case, the lookup value is the part number in column A of the Stock Status worksheet.

The second parameter, the compare vector, specifies the cell range to be searched — in this case, the compare vector is the column that contains the part numbers on the Raw Material worksheet.

The third and final parameter, the result vector, specifies the cell range containing the value that will be returned — in this case, the result vector is the column on the Raw Material worksheet that contains the part number descriptions.

The part number on the Stock Status worksheet is the lookup value, the range of cells A2 through A18 on the Raw Material worksheet is the compare vector, and the range of cells B2 through B18 on the Raw Material worksheet is the result vector.

The LOOKUP function searches for the first value in the compare vector that is equal to or less than the lookup value. So the correct description for each part number will be displayed in the cell next to each part number on the Stock Status worksheet *only if the part numbers on both worksheets are identical.*

Select cell B2 and enter the formula shown below, noting that a relative address is used for the lookup value to allow the formula to be copied into the remaining cells in column B.

=LOOKUP(A2,'Raw Material'!$A$2:$A$18,'Raw Material'!$B$2:$B$18)

The apostrophes (or single quotation marks, if you prefer) enclosing the worksheet name in this formula are required, because the worksheet name contains a space between the "w" in Raw and the "M" in Material.

When you enter this formula, the description for the part number shown in A2 will be taken from the Raw Material worksheet and displayed in cell B2 of the Stock Status worksheet as shown in Figure 4.3.

     File   Edit   Formula   Format   Data   Options   Macro   Window

| B2 | | =LOOKUP(A2,'Raw Material'!$A$2:$A$18,'Raw Material'! $B$2:$B$18) |

	A	B	C	D	E	F
1	Part No.	Description	On Order	Status		
2	100-00	Frame				
3	100-01					
4	100-02					
5	100-03					
6	100-04					
7	100-05					
8	100-06					
9	100-07					
10	100-08					
11	100-09					
12	200-01					
13	200-02					
14	300-00					
15	300-01					
16	300-02					
17	300-03					
18	300-04					
19						
20						

Figure 4.3 Results of the LOOKUP command on Stock Status worksheet

Although this formula works quite well under these circumstances, if the part numbers on the Raw Material worksheet are not in ascending order, the LOOKUP function can return the wrong description, since it returns the *first* value in the table that is equal to or *less than* the lookup value.

You can eliminate this problem by replacing the LOOKUP function with a compound formula. This formula consists of two functions that manipulate table data in a slightly different manner. The two functions in this compound formula are the MATCH and CHOOSE functions.

The MATCH function contains three parameters, known as the *lookup value*, the *compare value*, and the *type*. The first two parameters operate the same way the parameters used in the LOOKUP function do, but the third parameter is a number that specifies one of the three search conditions shown below.

Type	Condition
-1	smallest value that is greater than or equal to the lookup value
0	first value that is exactly equal to the lookup value
1	largest value that is less than or equal to the lookup value

Since no two part numbers are identical, if the type zero is specified, the MATCH function returns only one of two values: either a number that designates the *position* where the lookup value is located in the compare vector, or the error value #N/A if the lookup value does not match any of the entries in the compare vector.

For example, when you enter the formula shown below into cell B3 of the Stock Status worksheet, the number 2 is displayed, since part number 100-01 occupies the second position in the cell range A2 through A18 on the Raw Material worksheet.

= MATCH(A3,'Raw Material'!$A$2:$A$18,0)

Instead of returning the position of an item within a table, the CHOOSE function returns the *contents* of a particular cell within a given range of cells, based on what is called the *index value*.

In the *Excel User's Guide*, the CHOOSE function is depicted as CHOOSE (index,value-1,value-2,...). The term *cell range* will be used here instead of "value-1,value-2," since the CHOOSE command is normally used to return a value from a specified cell range instead of a set of predetermined values.

By using the value returned by the MATCH function as the *index* value for the CHOOSE function, you can ensure that the correct description for each part number will always be displayed.

To obtain the correct descriptions of the remaining part numbers, enter the compound formula shown below into cell B2 of the Stock Status worksheet, then copy it into cells B3 through B18.

= CHOOSE(MATCH(B2,'Raw Material'!$A$2:$A$18),
'Raw Material'!$B$2:$B$18)

Using this compound, you need not worry if the part numbers are not arranged in ascending order, since the entire list will be searched until an exact match is made. Further, any part number that does not appear on the Raw Material worksheet is easily identified, since the error value #N/A will appear in the descriptions column.

There is another option you can use that is equally effective and much easier to enter and use. It is also a compound command, and it uses the value returned by the MATCH function as the index value for the INDEX command.

The INDEX command contains three parameters (the *search range*, the *row index*, and the *column index*). The search range is the range of cells to be searched; the row index specifies the row containing the cell; and the column index specifies the number of columns to the left or right that contain the information that will be returned.

For example, if the named definition *RawMatl* on the Stock Status worksheet were defined as the cell range $A$2:$A$18 on the Raw Material worksheet, then entering the command shown in Figure 4.4 into B3 and copying it into cells B4:B18 will retrieve the description of each part number.

		File	Edit	Formula	Format	Data	Options	Macro	Window	

B3	=INDEX(RawMatl,MATCH(A3,'Raw Material'!$A$2:$A$18,0) ,2)

	A	B	C	D	E	F
1	Part No.	Description	On Order	Status		
2	100-00	Frame				
3	100-01	Handlebars				
4	100-02	Hardware Package				
5	100-03	Pedal, Left			✛	
6	100-04	Pedal, Right				
7	100-05	Rim, Front				
8	100-06	Rim, Rear				
9	100-07	Reflector, Red				
10	100-08	Tire, Standard				
11	100-09	Seat				
12	200-01	Fender, Front				
13	200-02	Fender, Rear				
14	300-00	Light				
15	300-01	Mirror				
16	300-02	Reflector, Amber				
17	300-03	Reflector, White				
18	300-04	Tire, Off Road				
19						
20						

Figure 4.4 Use of the INDEX command to retrieve information from the Raw Material worksheet

The entries that will appear in column C (which is titled On Order) will be maintained by the as-yet-uncreated PO macro, so for the time being leave these cells blank.

The Status column uses the information on the Raw Material worksheet as a fixed table to determine if a particular item is at or below its reorder point. If so, three asterisks are displayed in the cell; otherwise, nothing is displayed. This method makes it easy to identify quickly any low stock levels without having to compare the quantity in stock for every stock item with its reorder point.

If the asterisks appear, the user can check the corresponding entry in column C to see if sufficient quantities have been ordered or take other appropriate action.

While you can use several different techniques to determine if the stock level for each inventory item is below an acceptable level, the easiest technique uses simple external references within the IF function.

Select cell D2 and enter the formula shown below, making sure you enter the correct number of quotation marks where necessary.

$$= \text{IF('Raw Material'!}\$D\$2 <= \text{'Raw Material'!}\$E\$2, \text{"***","")}$$

If the three asterisks are not enclosed in quotation marks, Excel will attempt to evaluate them as a math formula instead of text, and it will display an error dialog box when you try to enter the formula.

The last two quotation marks in the formula *do not* have a space between them. This is known as a *null* string, and is the equivalent of entering *nothing* into the cell.

This formula simply compares the value found in cell D2 with the value contained in cell E2 on the Raw Material worksheet to determine if the value in D2 is less than or equal to the value in E2. If this is true, the three asterisks will be displayed; otherwise, the null string (or nothing) will appear in the cell.

This particular formula works as long as the part number displayed in row two of the Raw Material worksheet agrees with the part number displayed in row two of the Stock Status worksheet.

If either part number is moved to a different location, however, the results of the formula will be invalid. And since this formula uses absolute addressing, it cannot be copied to the remaining cells in the Stock Status worksheet.

You can overcome this limitation by creating a formula that uses named references instead of cell addresses. This formula is based on what is known as *equivalent position* — the value to be returned is located in the same position in the second table. Since named references are used, the formula can easily be copied into the cells of the Stock Status worksheet.

Select cell D3 on the Stock Status worksheet and enter the following formula.

= IF('Raw Material'!In_Stock< = 'Raw Material'!RO_Point,"***","")

Like the last formula, which used absolute addressing, this formula compares the quantity found in the column named In_Stock to the quantity found in the column named RO_Point, both of which are located on the Raw Material worksheet.

Based on equivalent positions, this formula compares the values that appear in the same row of the two worksheets. For example, since the formula is entered into D3 on the Stock Status worksheet, the comparison will be made based on the information in row three of the Raw Material worksheet, regardless of the part numbers.

As such, you can copy the formula into cells D3 through D18 on the Stock Status worksheet, and every time a recalculation is performed, any stock items at or below their reorder points will be flagged, as shown in Figure 4.5.

⌘ File Edit Formula Format Data Options Macro Window

D2	=IF('Raw Material'!In_Stock<='Raw Material'!RO_Point,"***","")

	A	B	C	D	E	F
1	Part No.	Description	On Order	Status		
2	100-00	Frame				
3	100-01	Handlebars				
4	100-02	Hardware Package				
5	100-03	Pedal, Left				
6	100-04	Pedal, Right		***		
7	100-05	Rim, Front		***		
8	100-06	Rim, Rear				
9	100-07	Reflector, Red				
10	100-08	Tire, Standard				
11	100-09	Seat				
12	200-01	Fender, Front				
13	200-02	Fender, Rear				
14	300-00	Light		***		
15	300-01	Mirror				
16	300-02	Reflector, Amber				
17	300-03	Reflector, White				
18	300-04	Tire, Off Road				
19						
20						

Figure 4.5 Using equivalent positions comparison to indicate items that need to be reordered

If any stock items are added or deleted, however, the formula may not give correct results, because the part numbers may not appear in the same rows on the two worksheets.

On the plus side, the formula takes only moments to create and is easy to update. Copy the part numbers and descriptions from the Raw Material worksheet, paste them into the Stock Status worksheet, and copy the formula into any new cells.

Parts List Worksheet

The next worksheet in the application is the Parts List worksheet, and it appears in Figure 4.6. The Parts List worksheet accesses the data on the Raw Material worksheet to create a parts listing for several products, using the VLOOKUP, INDEX, and MATCH commands in an array environment.

When completed, the Parts List worksheet will automatically compute the cost of each product, obtain the description and cost from the Raw Material worksheet based on the part number entered in column B, and show the quantity of parts entered in column D.

	A	B	C	D	E	F
1	Model	Part No.	Description	Quantity	Cost	
2	Tourister					
3						
4						
5						
6						
7						
8						
9						
10						
11						
12						
13						
14						
15						
16						
17						
18						
19						
20						

Figure 4.6 Parts List Worksheet

Enter all information shown on the worksheet in Figure 4.6, except for the descriptions and cost. Then use the Define Name option of the Formula menu to define

= 'Raw Material'!RawMat!

as shown in Figure 4.7. This definition will allow access to the data contained on the Raw Material worksheet.

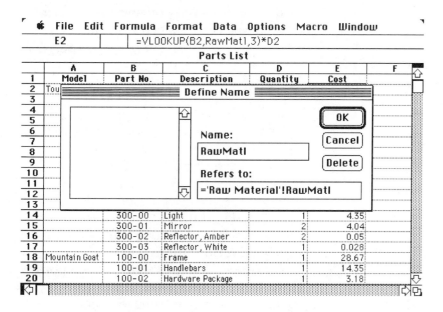

Figure 4.7 RawMatl defined on the parts list worksheet

To obtain the description of each part number for the Parts List worksheet, you can use a variation of the INDEX function with the MATCH function to form a compound command.

This variation of the INDEX function is shown in the *Excel User's Guide* as INDEX (array,row,column), and is described as the least preferred version of the function, although no explanation of *why* it's the least preferred is given (I've found it to be particularly useful). This variation of INDEX returns the value of a single cell within the cell range specified by the row and column values. As such, you use the row and column values to *index* the array. (Note: An array in this function does not require that you use the Command key, since the *array* is nothing more than a cell range.)

Select cell B2 on the Parts List worksheet and enter the formula shown below, which will obtain the description for each part number from the Raw Material worksheet, based on the part number shown in the Stock Status worksheet.

= INDEX(RawMatl,MATCH(A2,'Raw Material'!$A$2:$A$18,0),0,2)

Notice that the named reference RawMatl refers to a definition on the Raw Material worksheet that has an identical name. RawMatl could have been replaced with either

'Raw Material'!RawMatl

or

'Raw Material'!$A$2:$A$18

in either case, a single-dimension array. This array — A2 through A18 on the Raw Material worksheet — is the cell range that will be indexed.

The second portion of the command uses the exact match option of the **MATCH** function to determine the position of the part number. It finds the position of the part number by searching the Raw Material worksheet for the part number that appears in cell A2 on the Stock Status worksheet. This function returns the value 2, which is the row index value.

An external address is used to demonstrate that you can mix different forms of addressing in the same formula, even if both addressing forms refer to the same location.

The last number that appears in the formula, immediately before the closing parenthesis, is the column index value, also a 2. If you find the cell that appears in the second row and second column of the cell range A2 through E18 on the Raw Material worksheet, you'll find that it is the description for the part number found in cell A2 of the Stock Status worksheet. And since the **MATCH** command uses relative addressing for the lookup value, copying the formula to the remaining cells in column B of the Stock Status worksheet will provide the descriptions for all part numbers.

Finally, you determine the total cost of the parts used on each bicycle by obtaining the unit cost of each part number from the Raw Material worksheet, then multiplying it by the quantity that appears in column D. Do this by using the **VLOOKUP** function, the vertical lookup command, which locates an item in one column and returns a value in the same row from another column.

Select cell E2 and enter the formula shown below, noting that two relative addresses and one named reference are all that are required.

= VLOOKUP(B2,RawMatl,3)*D2

The vertical lookup command requires three parameters, the *lookup value,* the *compare array,* and the *index number.* The lookup value, as before, is the value you're searching for and in this instance is the part number located in column B.

The compare array (RawMatl, in this case) is the cell range to be searched for the largest value that is *less than* or *equal to* the lookup value. The index number specifies which column in the compare array the corresponding entry will be taken from.

Since the name *RawMatl* refers to cells A2 through E18 on the Raw Material worksheet, and since the value to be returned is located in the third column (which is titled *Cost*) of that range, an index value of 3 is used to specify the third column.

Once the VLOOKUP function obtains the cost for the part number, the cost is multiplied by the value found in column D to provide the total cost. Since relative addresses are used in the formula, you can copy the formula to the remaining cells in column E. This provides the total cost for each product, as shown in Figure 4.8.

	File	**Edit**	**Formula**	**Format**	**Data**	**Options**	**Macro**	**Window**

E2	=VLOOKUP(B2,RawMatl,3)*D2

Parts List

	A	B	C	D	E	F
1	Model	Part No.	Description	Quantity	Cost	
2	Tourister	100-00	Frame	1	28.67	
3		100-01	Handlebars	1	14.35	
4		100-02	Hardware Package	1	3.18	
5		100-03	Pedal, Left	1	0.43	
6		100-04	Pedal, Right	1	0.43	
7		100-05	Rim, Front	1	2.87	
8		100-06	Rim, Rear	1	3.12	
9		100-07	Reflector, Red	3	0.06	
10		100-08	Tire, Standard	2	3.06	
11		100-09	Seat	1	2.96	
12		200-01	Fender, Front	1	3.05	
13		200-02	Fender, Rear	1	3.69	
14		300-00	Light	1	4.35	
15		300-01	Mirror	2	4.04	
16		300-02	Reflector, Amber	2	0.05	
17		300-03	Reflector, White	1	0.028	
18	Mountain Goat	100-00	Frame	1	28.67	
19		100-01	Handlebars	1	14.35	
20		100-02	Hardware Package	1	3.18	

Figure 4.8 Parts List after VLOOKUP

Price List Worksheet

The next step you'll take is to create a Price List worksheet for all of the products, making further use of the information on the worksheets you've already created. One of the benefits of successively building on your worksheets is that whenever the cost of your raw material changes, all other worksheets — including the Price List — will be immediately updated.

Create the Price List worksheet shown in Figure 4.9 by entering the desired percentage increase over the cost (to obtain the selling price) in cells E1 through F3. Next, enter the titles shown in cells A1 through C1 and the models shown in A2 and A3.

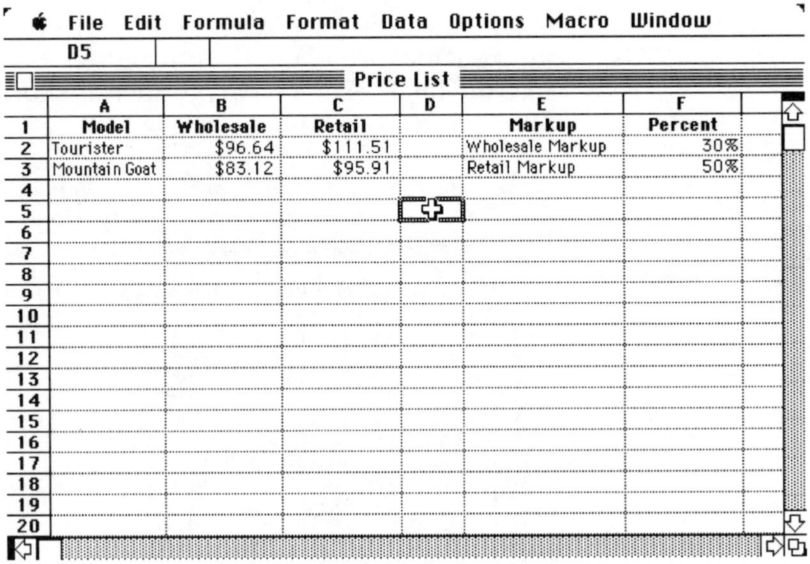

Figure 4.9 Price List worksheet

After you've entered the titles and models, define the two names shown below on the Parts List worksheet. These are the names of each model. Use the **SUM** function to obtain the total retail price.

Name	Refers to:
Tourister	= SUM($E$2:$E$17)
Mountain_Goat	= SUM($E$18:$E$28)

After you've defined *Tourister* and *Mountain_Goat*, select cell B2 and enter the formula

= 'Parts List'!Tourister*(1 + $F$2)

This formula uses the total cost of the Tourister bicycle provided by the name *Tourister* and then multiplies it by the value in F2 plus one —the equivalent of 130%.

It is important to enclose the portion of the formula that performs the addition in parentheses to obtain the correct figure. Otherwise, the formula would first multiply the total cost times one, then add 0.3 to it — obviously not a thirty-percent markup.

The wholesale price for the Mountain_Goat bicycle is obtained by substituting the name *Mountain_Goat* for *Tourister* in the formula.

To obtain the retail prices, substitute $F$3 for $F$2 in both formulas, entering them into the correct cells.

This formula will automatically increase or decrease the wholesale and retail prices of the bicycles if the cost of any part contained in the Raw Material worksheet is changed.

Understanding Arrays

Understanding what arrays are isn't nearly as difficult as understanding how they're used to simplify and enhance your worksheets. In essence, an array is nothing more than a cell range — be it several cells in a single column, the cells spanning multiple columns but limited to one row, or a combination of multiple rows and columns. Thus, an array can be the cell range B3:D5, the column named Description, or even the entire Raw Material worksheet.

Arrays give you the capability to perform calculations and functions that result in more than just a single value. Naturally, to get an array of values, the currently selected cell range must be larger than a single cell.

For example, to obtain the part numbers appearing in column A of the Stock Status worksheet, you've been copying all of the values from the Raw Material worksheet and pasting them into the Stock Status worksheet. With an array, this procedure of copying and pasting can be replaced with a single command entered into cell A2 of the Stock Status worksheet.

First, you must activate the Stock Status worksheet and select cells A2 through A18. Next, enter the formula shown below into cell A2 (first make sure that the cell range is still selected), but *do not* press Return or Enter or click the Enter box on the Formula bar.

= 'Raw Material'!$A$2:$A$18

After you have typed the formula, hold down the Command key *while* you either press the Enter key or click the Enter box on the Formula bar. Holding down the Command key while you press Enter tells Excel that this formula is an array formula, which must be treated as a single entity.

As soon as you enter this formula, all of the part numbers on the Raw Material worksheet are dynamically linked to the Stock Status worksheet in the same order that they appear in the Raw Material worksheet.

If you examine the formula now displayed in the Formula bar, you'll see it appears as:

{ = 'Raw Material'!$A$2:$A$18}

The braces, the symbols { and }, are the only indication you have that this entry is an array formula. Further, if you edit the contents of the cell for any reason, you *must hold down the Command key* when you press the Enter key or click the Enter box on the Formula bar. If you don't, the formula will not be considered an array formula, and it will not work.

This array contains entries in 17 rows but only one column, so it is known as a 17-by-1 array (the first number indicates the number of rows, the second the number of columns). An array extending from A1 through E4 would be a 4-by-5 array, because it includes four rows and five columns.

You can use arrays in formulas just as if they were normal cell references, as long as you hold down the command key when you enter the formula. For example, select F2 through F18 on the Raw Material worksheet and enter the formula shown below into cell F2, being sure to hold down the Command key while you enter the formula.

$$= C2:C18*D2:D18$$

This formula displays the total value of each part number currently in stock in the corresponding cells in column F. Thus, arrays provide multiple results from single formulas, while non-array items return a single result from a single formula.

One of the most useful features of arrays is the TRANSPOSE function. This function allows you to take an array that is primarily horizontally oriented (say a 4-by-5 array) and change it into one that is primarily vertically oriented (a 5-by-4 array).

So, if you have data in a row on one worksheet and need to place it in a column on another worksheet, the TRANSPOSE function can do it automatically.

For example, create the worksheet named *Array1* that is shown in Figure 4.10, then open a new worksheet and name it *Array2*.

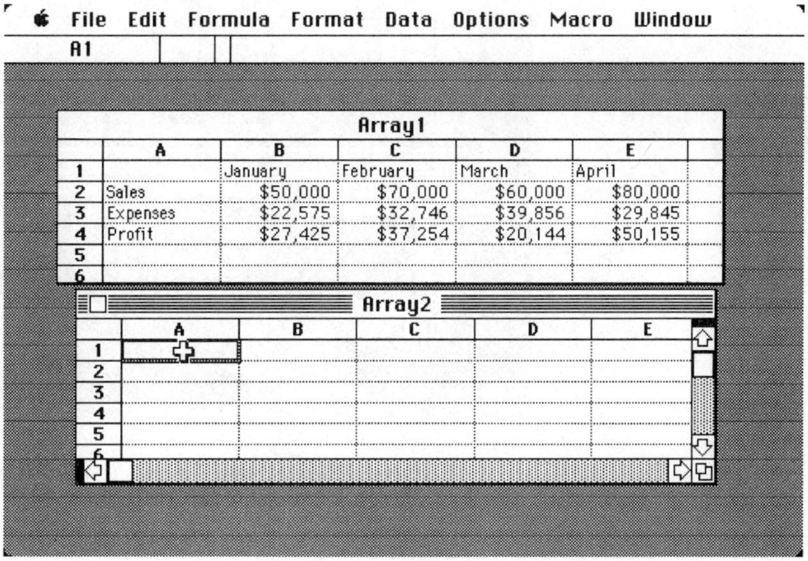

Figure 4.10 Array worksheets for transposing data

Next, select cells A1 through D5 on the worksheet named Array2 and type in the formula shown below. Make sure you hold down the Command key when you press Enter.

= TRANSPOSE(Array1!$A$1:$E$4)

When you press Enter, the entire array of cells A1 through E4 of the Array1 worksheet is transposed to the Array2 worksheet and occupies cells A1 through D5 (see Figure 4.11). Notice that the titles Sales, Expenses, and Profit now appear in B1 through D1 instead of A2 through A4.

If you're wondering where the zero came from that appears in cell A1 of the Array2 worksheet, the answer is that any blank cells are treated as the numeric value zero. To prevent the zero from showing up, select A1 on the Array1 worksheet, press the Space bar, then press the Enter key. (You also could have entered the formula = "" to simulate a null string, but it's much easier to press the Space bar, which replaces the zero with a space.)

| | File | Edit | Formula | Format | Data | Options | Macro | Window |

A1   {=TRANSPOSE(Array1!$A$1:$E$4)}

Array1

	A	B	C	D	E
1		January	February	March	April
2	Sales	$50,000	$70,000	$60,000	$80,000
3	Expenses	$22,575	$32,746	$39,856	$29,845
4	Profit	$27,425	$37,254	$20,144	$50,155
5					
6					

Array2

	A	B	C	D	E
1		0 Sales	Expenses	Profit	
2	January	$50,000	$22,575	$27,425	
3	February	$70,000	$32,746	$37,254	
4	March	$60,000	$39,856	$20,144	
5	April	$80,000	$29,845	$50,155	
6					

Figure 4.11 Array worksheets after the TRANSPOSE command

You can use the TRANSPOSE command to combine the figures on multiple worksheets by embedding a math formula within the parentheses of the TRANSPOSE command. Doing this will allow you to compute multiple values before transposing them to another worksheet.

Open a third worksheet named Array3 and enter the information shown in Figure 4.12. You'll use this method to combine the values with the TRANSPOSE command.

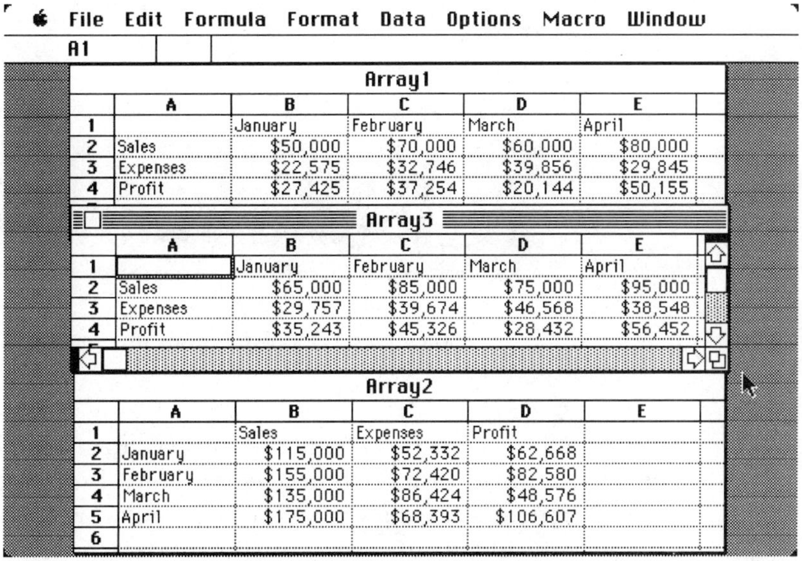

Figure 4.12 Array3 worksheet

You would normally expect that the data from worksheets Array1 and Array3 could be combined if you simply selected cells A1 through D5 on the Array2 worksheet and entered the formula shown below.

$$= \text{TRANSPOSE}(\text{Array1!\$A\$1:\$E\$4} + \text{Array3!\$A\$1:\$E\$4})$$

If this formula is entered as shown, Excel will add the numbers appearing in cells B2 through E4 of both the Array1 and Array3 worksheets and correctly display them in cells B2 through D5 of the Array2 worksheet. Unfortunately, it will also attempt to add the titles, which will result in the error figures shown in Figure 4.13.

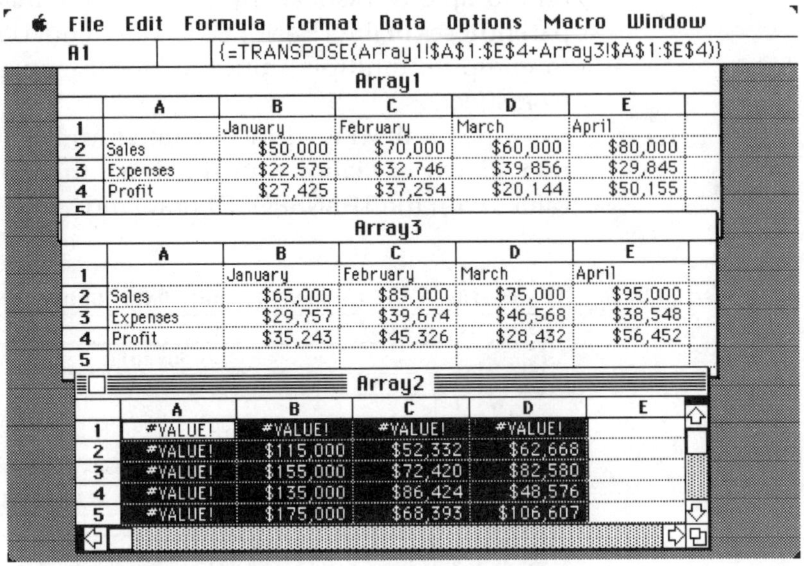

Figure 4.13 Error figures from attempting to add worksheet titles

To add and combine these values, you must use three different array formulas. First, select cells A1 through D5 on the Array2 worksheet and press Command-B, which is the equivalent of choosing the Blank option of the Edit menu and which will delete the contents of the cell.

Next, select cells B1 through D1 on the Array2 worksheet and enter the formula shown below to transpose the titles that appear in column A of the Array1 worksheet.

=TRANSPOSE(Array1!$A$2:$A$4)

To transpose the names of the months that appear in B1 through E1, select A2 through A5 on the Array2 worksheet and enter the following.

=TRANSPOSE(Array1!$B$1:$E$1)

Finally, to add and transpose the figures from both the Array1 and Array3 worksheets occupying cells B2 through E4, select cells B2 through D5 on the Array2 worksheet and enter the formula shown below.

=TRANSPOSE(Array1!$B$2:$E$4 + Array3!$B$2:$E$4)

By using three array formulas, you can combine the information from two different worksheets into a third with much less effort than would be required if you used individual formulas. Figure 4.14 shows the results of the three transposition operations.

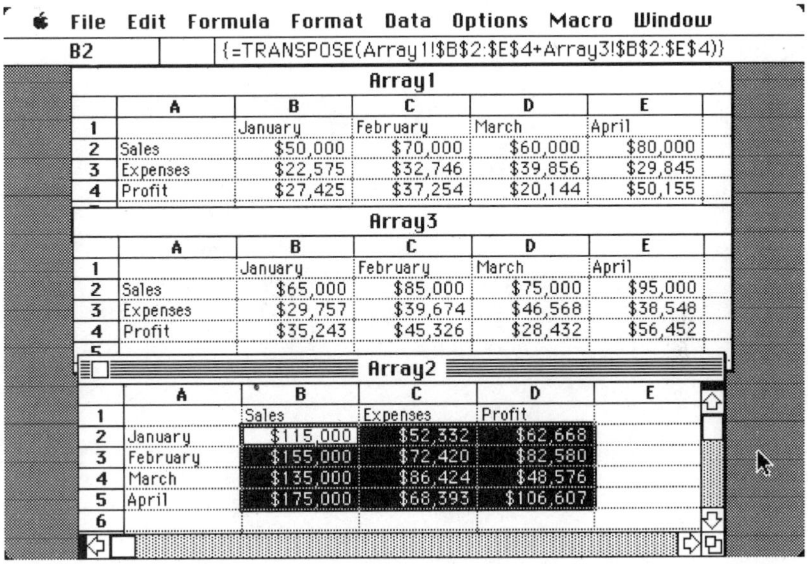

Figure 4.14 Results of transpose functions

Summary

In this chapter, you used both fixed tables and arrays as tables to access and manipulate large quantities of data with only one or two commands. You saw how these functions not only simplify your worksheets, but increase their speed as well.

You used arrays to transpose data from one worksheet to another, perform multiple calculations simultaneously, and reduce the number of commands required to manipulate large quantities of data.

CHAPTER

5

Database and Criteria

In reality, Excel has no database. What most people perceive to be a database is actually nothing more than a named cell range. And although the cell range must be organized in a specific format for access by the eight special data manipulation commands, you do not need to access either the Set Database or Set Criteria options of the Data menu to create a database area.

This chapter dispels the myths and misconceptions surrounding Excel's database and criteria areas (the terms are used for consistency). You'll learn how to create several active database and criteria areas on one worksheet instead of having to constantly designate an active database area. You'll learn how to use one criteria area for multiple database areas. Finally, you'll learn how to take advantage of the vaguely defined options associated with the eight special-purpose commands designed expressly for data manipulation.

Multiple Database Areas

Incorporating multiple database areas into your worksheets increases the data manipulation capabilities available to you and lets you keep your data segregated. You can take advantage of these capabilities by understanding what happens when a database range is defined.

65

Create the worksheet shown in Figure 5.1, which contains the sales and expenses of four regional offices, named North, East, South, and West. Notice that the organization of each cell range on the worksheet meets Excel's requirements for a database: field names appear in the first row of each cell range; all information concerning a specific entry is contained in a single row.

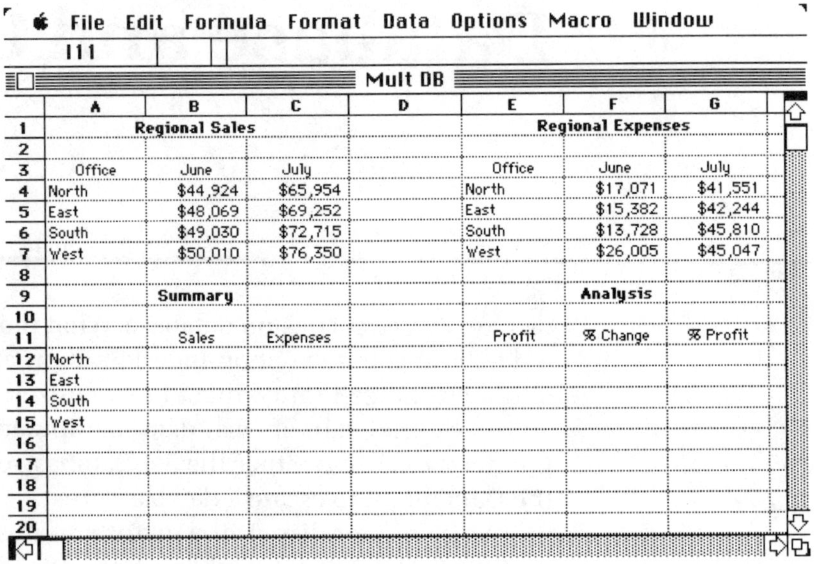

	A	B	C	D	E	F	G
1		Regional Sales				Regional Expenses	
2							
3	Office	June	July		Office	June	July
4	North	$44,924	$65,954		North	$17,071	$41,551
5	East	$48,069	$69,252		East	$15,382	$42,244
6	South	$49,030	$72,715		South	$13,728	$45,810
7	West	$50,010	$76,350		West	$26,005	$45,047
8							
9		Summary				Analysis	
10							
11		Sales	Expenses		Profit	% Change	% Profit
12	North						
13	East						
14	South						
15	West						
16							
17							
18							
19							
20							

Figure 5.1 Mult DB worksheet

Next, select cells A3 through C7 and choose the Set Database option of the Data menu, as you would normally, to define the area as a database.

After defining the database area, immediately choose the Define Name option of the Formula menu and click the name *Database*. When you do this, you'll see that the name *Database* now refers to cells $A$3:$C$7.

Thus, selecting the Set Database option of the Data menu simply assigns the name *Database* to the currently selected cell range. Once you understand that a database area is nothing more than a named cell range, you can create as many database areas on a single worksheet as you need. All you must do is define a different name for each database area with the Define Name (or Create Name) option of the Formula menu.

The next step is to take advantage of the options associated with the eight database functions that let you access and manipulate the data in each database area.

First, delete the named reference *Database* by choosing the Delete option of the Define Name menu, then establish a new name for one of the two database areas on this worksheet. Select cells A3 through C7, choose the Define Name option of the Formula menu, then enter the definition shown in Figure 5.2.

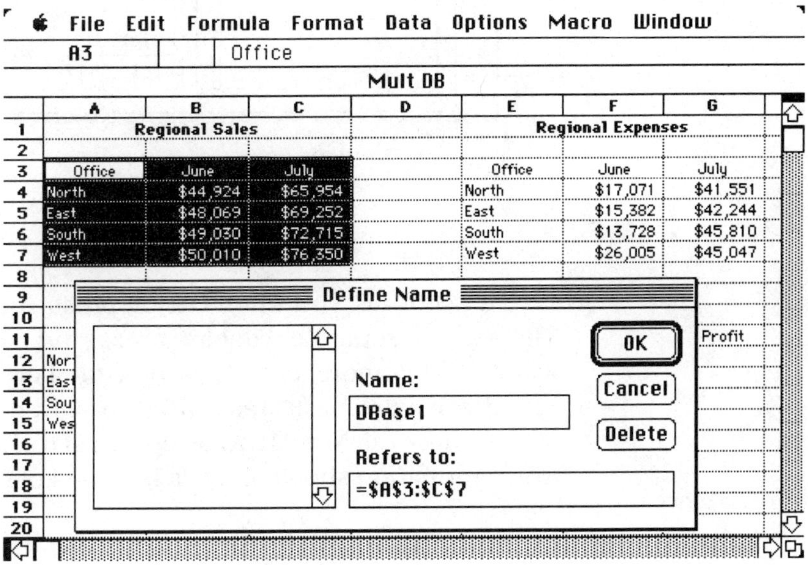

Figure 5.2 DBase1 defined

This defines the name DBase1 as a cell range that contains the sales made during the months of June and July for each regional office.

Next, create a second database area by selecting cells E3 through G7. Again, choose the Define Name option of the Formula menu and enter the definition shown in Figure 5.3.

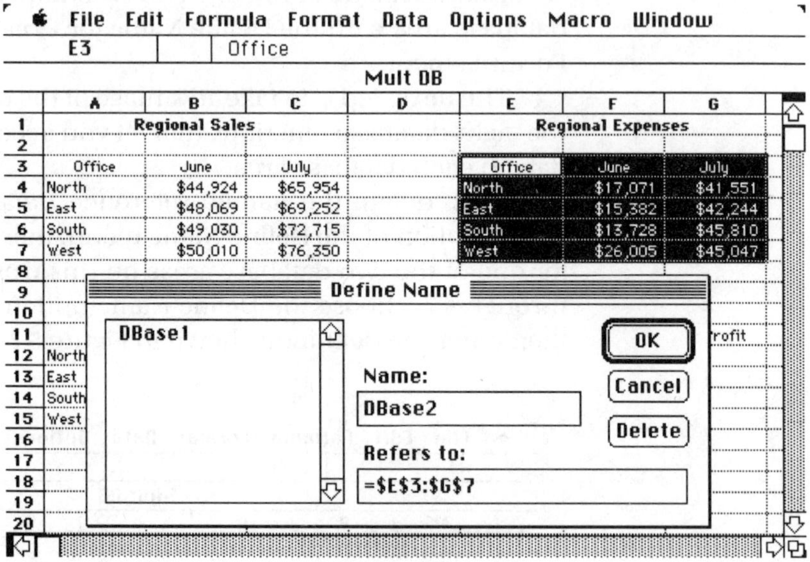

Figure 5.3 DBase2 defined

As soon as you click OK or press the Return key, you have defined two separate database areas, and both database areas (there can be many more) are active. A criteria area is all that you need to use the two database areas with the eight database commands.

Choose the New Window option of the Window menu and enter the information shown in cells I3 and I4 of Figure 5.4.

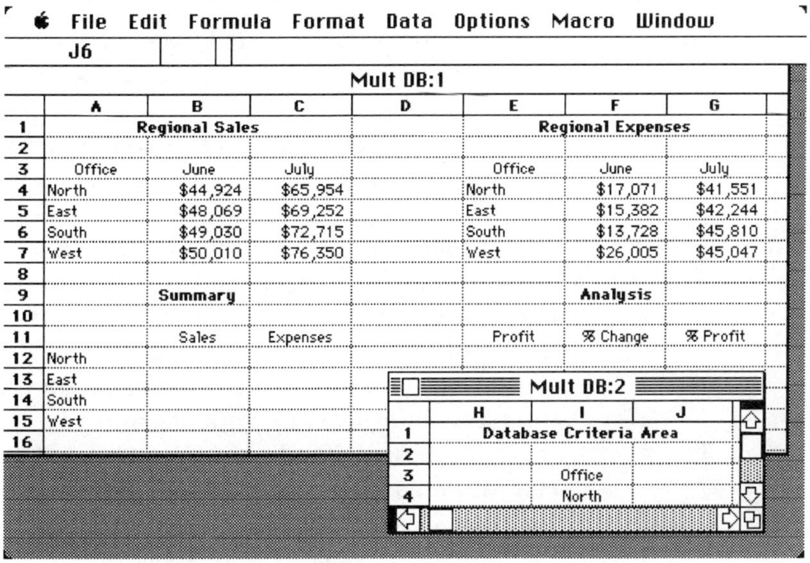

Figure 5.4 Criteria area for Mult DB worksheet

After you've entered the data, select both cells and then choose the Set Criteria option of the Data menu. This assigns the name *Criteria* to the selected cells, just as the Set Database option assigned the name *Database*.

Now, you are ready to use the options associated with Excel's database commands to access and manipulate the data in the databases.

Database Command Options

Every database command in Excel has three options associated with it, shown in the *Excel User's Guide* as *Database,* *field name* or *field index*, and *Criteria*.

The name *Database* refers to any named cell range that meets the requirements for a database area, such as DBase1 and DBase2. The next parameter, called *field name* or *field index*, designates a particular column of cells within the database that will be used as the argument for a database command. For example, if you wanted to find all sales less than $48,500, you would use the number 48000 as the argument for either the June or July sales.

The last option, named *Criteria,* refers to a cell range containing the name of at least one specification for a field. You normally use this by entering a field name into one cell and its argument into the cell immediately below it, then choosing the Set Criteria option of the Data Menu.

Since both DBase1 and DBase2 conform to these rules, you can use both names with any database command by substituting their names for the term *Database*.

The field index uses a number to designate a particular field. The first field in the database (Office, in this example) is referenced by 1; the second (July) is referenced by 2; and so on. You can, of course, use the actual field name by enclosing it in quotation marks.

So, to obtain the total of all values in the field named June for the North office in the cell range named DBase1, you would enter the formula

$$= DSUM(DBase1,``June",Criteria)$$

into any cell on the worksheet. It specifies the database area (DBase1), the field name (June), and the criteria area (Criteria).

For example, obtain the total sales for the North office by selecting cell B12 and entering the compound formula shown in the Formula bar of Figure 5.5.

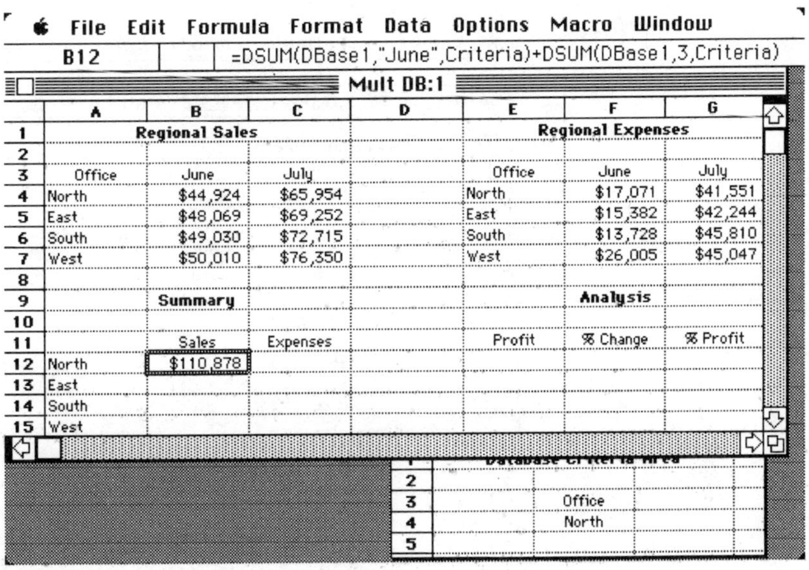

Figure 5.5 Compound database command to obtain total sales for North office

Notice that the first portion of the formula uses a field name, while the second part of the formula uses a field index. You can use either method with equally successful results, or you can even combine both, as has been done here.

Next, obtain the expenses for the North office that appear in DBase2 by selecting cell C12 and substituting the name DBase2 for DBase1 in the formula, as shown in Figure 5.6.

	File Edit Formula Format Data Options Macro Window						

G21

Mult DB

	A	B	C	D	E	F	G
1		Regional Sales				Regional Expenses	
2							
3	Office	June	July		Office	June	July
4	North	$44,924	$65,954		North	$17,071	$41,551
5	East	$48,069	$69,252		East	$15,382	$42,244
6	South	$49,030	$72,715		South	$13,728	$45,810
7	West	$50,010	$76,350		West	$26,005	$45,047
8							
9		Summary				Analysis	
10							
11		Sales	Expenses		Profit	% Change	% Profit
12	North						
13	East						
14	South						
15	West						
16							
17							
18							
19							
20							

Figure 5.6 Compound database command to obtain total expenses for North office

As you can see, both database areas are active and operate as if you had chosen the Set Database command and were using only one database area. Obviously, you can discover many excellent features of Excel simply by exploring the alternatives that are not explicitly given in the *Excel User's Guide*. The use of multiple database areas was discovered in this manner.

Shared Criteria

Perhaps you've noticed that the name *Criteria* appears in both parts of the formula, even though each function refers to a different database area. This technique of using *shared criteria* is made possible by the careful selection of the field names that appear in both database areas. You can use shared criteria to reduce the number of criteria areas, to increase calculation time, and to simplify your worksheets.

When you use shared criteria, make sure the field names are identical in both database areas. Otherwise, everything may appear to be operating correctly, but you'll be manipulating the data in only one database.

Thus, you can establish a criteria area for use by more than one database — regardless of its name — provided that the field names used in the criteria area appear in both database areas and are identical.

Multiple Criteria

By applying the same theory used to obtain multiple database areas on a single worksheet, you can establish several different criteria areas that any or all active database areas can use. Many times you can use this technique in lieu of Excel's TABLE function to increase the speed of your applications by as much as 50 percent.

You can also use multiple criteria areas to provide an instant summary of specific portions of your worksheet. Take, for example, the common application of a check register. A check register is commonly used to provide a record of payments made and the current balance, but you can establish multiple criteria areas that automatically summarize your expenditures by category.

Create the Check Register worksheet by entering the data shown in Figure 5.7 and defining cells A1 through E12 as a database area assigned the name *Checks*. (All values enclosed in parentheses are entered as negative values, such as -1253.35, and are formatted as dollars via the Number option of the Format menu.)

	A	B	C	D	E	F
	Check No.	Date	Memoranda	Category	Amount	
1	1001	9/10/86	First National Bank	A1	($1,253.35)	
2	1002	9/11/86	Office Supply Co.	B1	($2,957.07)	
3	1003	9/12/86	Northern Distributors Inc.	C1	($5,834.21)	
4	1004	9/13/86	Eastern Distributors Inc.	C1	($6,584.13)	
5	1005	9/14/86	Good Office Supply	B1	($438.05)	
6		9/15/86	Deposit	DP	$37,958.65	
7	1006	9/16/86	Office Supply Co.	B1	($2,589.00)	
8	1007	9/17/86	Office Supply Co.	B1	($114.67)	
9	1008	9/18/86	Northern Distributors	C1	($8,736.94)	
10	1009	9/19/86	Eastern Distributors	C1	($4,399.85)	
11		9/20/86	Deposit	DP	$22,767.83	

Figure 5.7 Check Register worksheet

Next, open a second window by choosing the New Window option of the Window Menu. Then enter the information shown in Figure 5.8. The second window will be used to establish and monitor the criteria and summary areas for the Check Register worksheet.

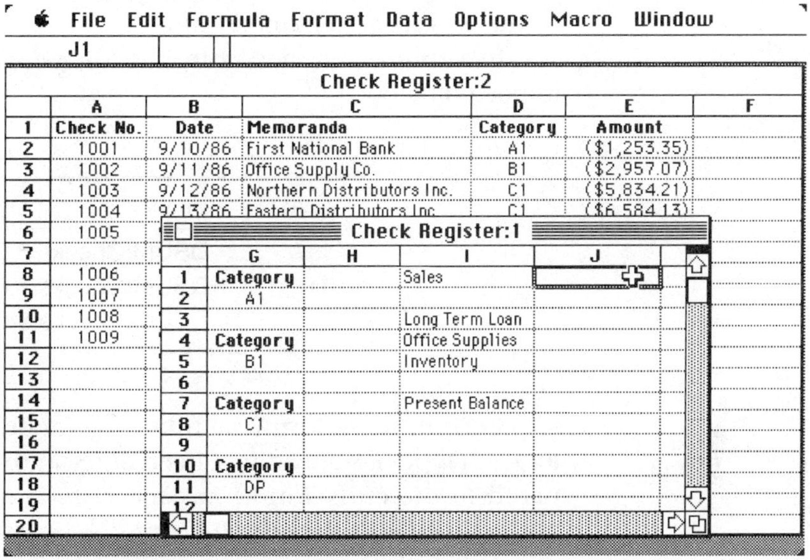

Figure 5.8 Criteria and summary areas for the Check Register worksheet

Using the Define Name option of the Formula menu, create several different criteria areas by assigning the names shown below to their respective cell ranges.

Name	Cell Range
Cat1	= $G$1:$G$2
Cat2	= $G$4:$G$5
Cat3	= $G$7:$G$8
Cat4	= $G$10:$G$11

These names will serve as the criteria for Long Term Loans, Office Supplies, Inventory, and Sales, respectively.

Next, select cell J1 and enter the formula shown below to total all deposits that appear on the worksheet.

= DSUM(Checks,5,Cat4)

This formula uses the field index option to total all transactions that have an entry in the Category field of DP (deposit), as specified by the criteria area named Cat4.

In a similar manner, enter the following formulas into the cells indicated below.

Cell	Formula
J3	= DSUM(Checks,5,Cat1)
J4	= DSUM(Checks,5,Cat2)
J5	= DSUM(Checks,5,Cat3)

Each of these formulas totals the amount of money disbursed for each type of transaction. Each entry in the Category field is compared to the entry found in each criteria area, and the totals are placed in cells J3 through J5.

Although the categories DP and A1 through C1 are used here, actual general ledger account numbers could be substituted for use in your accounting system or for export to another worksheet that may contain bugetary comparisons.

Finally, enter the formula

$$= SUM(J1,J3:J5)$$

into J7 to obtain the current balance. This figure is based on the *four active criteria areas*, since the figures that appear in J3:J5 are the result of the database commands that manipulate the data in those cells.

Computed Criteria

Computed criteria does not follow the conventional "database" methods used to establish criteria areas and is much closer to the methods used in non-database applications. Computed criteria uses conventional logic operands, like AND, OR, and NOT, in a formula that specifies the first cell in a particular field. When recalculation is performed, Excel will test every entry in the field to see if it meets the criteria.

Using computed criteria effectively in your applications is much easier when you understand something about the most commonly used logical operands and their results.

First, all logical operands evaluate to one of two states, TRUE or FALSE, and are the results of a comparison.

For example, suppose you were testing a series of values (such as check amounts) and wanted to find all items that were greater than $3,000.00 and less than $5,000.00. This establishes two comparisons, greater than three thousand AND less than five thousand; both of these comparisons must be satisfied before the number is added to the total.

If the number being tested passes the first comparison, the results are said to be TRUE. If it fails, the results are said to be FALSE. So, only if the results of both comparisons are true will the data meet the established criteria. Hence, it could be said that the results of the evaluations must be TRUE AND TRUE for the entire expression to be true.

In Excel, this TRUE AND TRUE comparison requires a slightly different syntax. First, the two values are enclosed within parentheses and separated by a comma. Second, an equal symbol and the word AND precedes the values enclosed in parentheses, resulting in a formula that reads: = AND (Comparison1,Comparison2).

Thus, you can find any check with an amount greater than $3,000.00 and less than $5,000.00 by entering the formula shown below into cell G2 on the Check Register worksheet.

$$= AND(\$E\$2>3000,\$E\$2<5000)$$

This formula will cause Excel to test every value in column E, beginning with cell E2, for values greater than 3,000 and less than 5,000. If any value is found that meets these requirements, the word TRUE will be displayed in the cell. If no value is found, the word FALSE will be displayed.

When this formula is used as criteria with a database command, such as the DSUM function, the number $4,399.85 — the only check that meets both requirements — will be displayed.

By constructing what is known as a truth table, it is easy to examine the different results possible for both comparisons and determine the final result provided by the AND function.

As shown in Figure 5.9, there are four possible combinations of the comparisons. If you examine each combination (reading across), you'll see that the only way the AND function will provide a logical TRUE is if the results of both comparisons are TRUE.

Comparison 1	Comparison 2	Result Value
TRUE	TRUE	TRUE
FALSE	TRUE	FALSE
TRUE	FALSE	FALSE
FALSE	FALSE	FALSE

Figure 5.9 AND truth table

Another frequently used logical operand is the OR function. Instead of requiring both comparisons to be true, the OR function requires that only one comparison is true for the entire expression to evaluate as true. So instead of being phrased as TRUE AND TRUE, the OR function is phrased as TRUE OR TRUE.

As you can see in the truth table shown in Figure 5.10, the overall result of TRUE will be obtained if either of the comparisons evaluates as TRUE.

Comparison 1	Comparison 2	Result Value
TRUE	TRUE	TRUE
FALSE	TRUE	TRUE
TRUE	FALSE	TRUE
FALSE	FALSE	FALSE

Figure 5.10 OR truth table

Even though there is only a minute difference between the AND and OR functions, the difference between them can have a major effect on your worksheets if they are used without careful consideration of their results.

For example, to extract the total amount of all money spent between September 12, 1986, and September 17, 1986, you can create computed criteria using the AND function that would appear as

$$= AND(\$B\$2 > 9/11/86, \$B\$2 < 9/17/86)$$

This formula would test the date each check was written to ensure that only those dates between September 12 and September 17 would be included.

If you used the OR function instead of the AND function, however, you would not total the checks written in just a five-day period, you would total *all* checks since the first comparison would include every check written after September 12, 1986, and the second comparison would include all checks written before September 17, 1986.

Quite frequently, locating all checks within a given time period isn't sufficient. For example, while you may need to find all checks written between September 12 and September 17, you may also want to limit the search to a specific category or to exclude a category. In these instances, you can create a conventional criteria area or you can use compound computed criteria.

For example, to extract all checks written between September 12 and September 17 and exclude all deposits, you can create a criteria area spanning six cells containing the following information.

Date	Date	Category
>9/11/86	<9/17/86	<>DP

This method causes all entries in the Date field to be evaluated twice: once, to ensure that the entry is greater than the numerical representation (all dates in Excel are numbers) of September 9, 1986; again, to ensure that the entry is less than September 17, 1986. Next, a third comparison is required to ensure that the entry in the Category field does not equal DP.

Every time a recalculation occurs, Excel must check six cells to determine if a particular check meets the criteria you have established, which in essence, is nothing more than a compound AND formula. For a value to be added, it must provide results of TRUE, TRUE, and TRUE for each comparison.

By using compound computed criteria, you can reduce the six cells to a single cell that contains the same criteria. Using one cell results in faster execution, since only one cell needs to be referenced during calculation.

To total all figures that are not deposits between September 12, 1986, and September 16, 1986, you can use a compound command consisting of two AND functions, as shown below.

=AND(AND($B$2>9/11/86,$B$2<9/17/86),$D$2<>DP)

The innermost AND function,

AND($B$2>9/11/86,$B$2<9/17/86)

which establishes the date limitations, becomes a part of the outermost AND function and provides a single logical value. If the date of any check is between September 12 and September 17, a value of TRUE will be established. If not, a value of FALSE will be returned.

The value returned by the innermost AND function then becomes the result of the first comparison for the outermost AND function.

The results of the first comparison are then combined with the restrictions for the category — the second comparison of the outermost AND function.

If all comparisons evaluate as TRUE, the value will be included in the total. But if any comparison evaluates as FALSE, the value will be excluded.

Any time you find you're establishing criteria areas that require several cells, you should use computed criteria instead. Not only will they increase the speed of your applications, computed criteria will reduce the amount of memory required, since there is less information for Excel to keep track of.

You can also create several computed (or noncomputed, for that matter) criteria areas, assign a single name to all of them, and use that name for extremely complex criteria.

Further, computed criteria does not have to be assigned a name to be used. You can include the cell reference directly in the database command where you normally place the criteria name. For example, the command

= DSUM(Database,1,$F$2)

would use the computed criteria found in cell F2.

When you're working with computed criteria (especially compound computed criteria), you must be sure that your logic — the ANDs, ORs, TRUEs, and FALSEs — will provide you with the results you're seeking. When in doubt, construct your own truth table expressly for the criteria you're using.

For example, a truth table for the compound AND function you used to extract all checks between September 12 and September 17 that were not deposits might appear as shown below.

>9/12/86	<9/17/86	<>DP	End Result
True	True	True	True
False	True	True	False
True	False	True	False
True	True	False	False

Once you've created your custom truth table, pick a few data samples at random and trace each one through your table.

Summary

In this chapter, you learned how to create more than one active database per worksheet, each with its own criteria area, to expand the data manipulation capabilities of your application.

You used a variety of criteria methods, including shared criteria, which can be used with more than one database to reduce the size of your applications.

You learned how to use computed criteria and logic operands to increase the speed of execution and to reduce the memory requirements of your worksheets. Computed criteria and logic operands can also require less time to write and test.

Properly used, all of these techniques will expand the effectiveness of your applications and the overall usefulness of Excel.

CHAPTER

6

Command Macros

Excel supports two different types of macros, command macros and function macros. Command macros are capable of taking the same actions that are available to you through either the keyboard or the mouse; in addition, they can return the results of a formula. Function macros cannot take any actions, however, and are special-purpose formulas you design that return a value.

Command macros can be used to automate many tasks, saving you both time and effort, while simultaneously reducing the possibility of errors. Further, since they have access to virtually every Excel function that you can normally perform, there is little you can't accomplish with a well-written command macro.

In this chapter, you'll learn the basic procedures, commands, and techniques required for creating successful macros. By actually writing command macros that perform specific functions on a worksheet, you'll understand how to select cells, format data, and enter formulas. Upon completion of this chapter, you'll know how the basics found in all macros can be used to accomplish meaningful tasks.

Once you understand how to create a command macro, you'll have virtually no trouble creating function macros, but with well over 80 predefined functions available, one must ask if a function macro is truly needed.

Macro Basics

Believe it or not, if you've used Excel to any extent, you already know well over 60 percent of the commands needed to create macros. Most of the commands used to create macros are the same commands you access through Excel's menus or enter into cells on a worksheet.

Further, since there is little difference between a macro sheet and a worksheet, you already have a reasonably good idea of how a macro sheet should be organized: data and commands are entered into individual cells, which form a complete application; calculation always begins with cell A1. The minor alternatives will be examined as they are encountered.

Macros — all macros — have the same general structure, follow the same sequence of execution, and share certain common elements that you can use to your advantage.

First, every command you enter on a macro sheet must begin with an equal symbol and will contain parentheses. Second, regardless of how you enter an command, when you press Return or Enter, the command will always be converted to uppercase, *unless it is incorrect!* So, by watching for any commands that don't appear in uppercase, you can quickly eliminate well over 85 percent of your typographical errors. Third, all macros must have a beginning and an ending cell and will execute commands going down the macro sheet from the beginning cell. The sequence can, however, be altered by use of special commands.

Common Procedures

Certain commands and procedures are used in almost every command macro. These very common macro commands and procedures include:

- selecting, formatting, and entry of data into cells
- controlling the sequence of execution (sometimes called the *flow of control*), and
- documenting and testing of macros

Examining these procedures now will let you focus your efforts on the more advanced operations needed to create and successfully implement macros in an integrated environment. The commands and procedures you'll examine first are the various techniques used to select cells on worksheets and macro sheets.

To select a cell or a range of cells on a worksheet, you use the SELECT command and follow it with the cell address, which is enclosed within parentheses.

For example, to select cell A1 on the currently active worksheet (not the macro sheet), you would use the following command.

$$= SELECT(!A1)$$

Notice the exclamation mark that precedes the cell address. When the exclamation mark is included, the command will select cell A1 on the currently active worksheet. When it's omitted, the same command will select cell A1 on the macro sheet. You can, of course, use full external references that include the name of the worksheet to avoid any confusion, although this will result in more typing and a macro that requires more memory.

The following examples show several variations commonly used with the SELECT command and their explanations.

Command	Explanation
= SELECT(!A1:B5)	selects cells A1 through B5 on the currently active worksheet
= SELECT(!A:A)	selects column A on the currently active worksheet
= SELECT(B5)	selects cell B5 on the currently active macro sheet
= SELECT(Loan!A1)	selects cell A1 on the worksheet named Loan

To enter any type of data into a cell, you would use the FORMULA command. If your entry is either text or a formula, you must enclose the text or formula in quotation marks, as shown below.

$$= FORMULA(\text{"Employee Name"})$$
$$= FORMULA(\text{"} = 2*Balance/Payment\text{"})$$

If your formula or function contains a cell address, however, you should use Excel's RC (Row/Column) style of addressing to enter the addresses in the formula. Failure to do so may result in an error while the macro is running and may prevent your formula from being entered into the cell.

For example, instead of entering

= FORMULA("= PMT($B$2,B3,B1)")

into your macro sheet, enter

= FORMULA("= PMT(R2C2,R3C2,R1C2)")

instead. Using RC addressing will prevent Excel from attempting to use the actual data that appears in the cells as part of the formula and ensures that cell addresses are used.

You can establish any data format you desire through the use of the ALIGNMENT, FORMAT.NUMBER (note the period separating the words), BORDER, and STYLE commands. These are the equivalent of Excel's menu selections, and in operation, they are very similar to their menu counterparts. All operate only on the currently selected cell range.

If you wanted to format a number that expresses all values as dollars and encloses negative figures in parentheses, you could use the following command.

= FORMAT.NUMBER("$#,###.00 ;($#,###.00)")

Using this command is the same as accessing the Number option of the Format menu, then entering a custom format. The $ symbol specifies that the first character displayed will always be the dollar sign; the # symbols indicate numbers; and the zeros specify that zeros are to be displayed if there is no other number.

To align data within a cell, you use a number to represent each of the five selections available when you choose the Alignment option of the Format menu. The first selection, General, is represented by a value of one; Left, Center, Right, and Fill are assigned the numbers two through five, respectively.

If you wanted to specify a center alignment, you would enter

= ALIGNMENT(3)

into the appropriate cell on your macro sheet. This specifies that the third option — center — of the Alignment selection is to be used.

Both the BORDER and STYLE commands use logical values (TRUE and FALSE) to specify which options are active and which are inactive. A value of TRUE means that the option is active, and a value of FALSE means that the option is inactive. As with the Alignment options, the Border and Style options are specified in the order that they appear in their respective menus.

For the BORDER command, the five items, in order, are: Outline, Left, Right, Top, and Bottom. So, entering a command that reads

=BORDER(FALSE,FALSE,FALSE,TRUE,TRUE)

would specify that the Top and Bottom options would be active, while the other three would be inactive.

For the STYLE command, you need to be concerned only with Bold and Italic. If you entered

=STYLE(TRUE,FALSE)

into a cell, the cell contents would be displayed in bold without italics.

Once you understand these basic commands, you have sufficient knowledge to create simple but useful macros that will automatically format your worksheets. In fact, you can use these commands to write a macro that will automatically create a Loan Information Template.

Use the New option of the File menu, choose Macro sheet, and click OK to place a new macro sheet on the desktop. Next, enter the information shown in Figure 6.1 to create a macro that will create a simple Loan Information worksheet.

	A
1	*Loan Macro*
2	=NEW(1)
3	=SELECT(!A1)
4	=FORMULA("Principal")
5	=SELECT(!A2)
6	=FORMULA("Interest Rate")
7	=SELECT(!A3)
8	=FORMULA("Term of Loan")
9	=SELECT(!A5)
10	=FORMULA("Monthly Payment")
11	*Establish Cell Formats*
12	=SELECT(!B1)
13	=FORMAT.NUMBER("$#,###.00")
14	=SELECT(!B2)
15	=FORMAT.NUMBER("0.00%")
16	=SELECT(!B3)
17	=FORMAT.NUMBER("##")
18	*Enter Payment Formula and Format*
19	=SELECT(!B5)
20	=FORMULA("=PMT(R2C2,R3C2,R1C2)")
21	=FORMAT.NUMBER("$#,###.00 ;($#,###.00)")
22	=RETURN()

Figure 6.1 Loan Information macro

Notice the entries that appear in cells A1, A11, and A18. These are known as "comments," or "remarks," and except for the space they occupy, they have absolutely no effect on the operation of the macro. You use them to provide gentle reminders about what the various portions of the macro do.

By displaying remarks in bold italics, you clearly separate them from each of the commands in the macro, making it fairly easy to identify what each portion of the macro (or routine) accomplishes.

After you've entered the information, choose the Define Name option of the Formula menu and enter the definition shown in Figure 6.2.

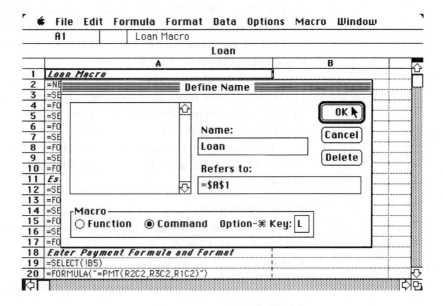

Figure 6.2 Naming a macro

By assigning the name *Loan* to cell A1, you've accomplish two things: you've designated the starting point for the macro, and you've used a name that makes it easy to remember what this particular macro does. You'll find this helpful when you're using more than one macro with a worksheet.

Next, you can open a new worksheet every time you want to use this macro, or you can use the NEW command that appears in A2. This command has three options that are used to specify the type of file to open, each indicated by a number enclosed in parentheses. Entering a 1 will open a new worksheet, entering a 2 will open a new chart, and entering a 3 will open a new macro sheet.

To start this or any other macro, you choose the Run option of the Macro menu. When the dialog box appears on your monitor, click on the name of the macro you want to run, then click OK. Here, you'll click the name *Macro1!Loan*, since that's the name you assigned to it.

When the macro starts, you'll see the new worksheet opened, each cell selected, the data and formulas entered, and the various formats established for each cell. When the macro ends, it returns control of your computer back to the keyboard (or mouse, or you, depending on your choice).

At this time, you have a template for determining the monthly payment of any loan by entering only three values: the principal (amount borrowed), the monthly interest rate entered as a decimal, and the term of the loan in months.

To make certain that the template works properly, simulate a loan of $1,000.00 at a yearly interest rate of 12% over a period of three years by entering:

- 1000 into cell B1
- .01 into cell B2 (divide the yearly interest rate by 12 to obtain the monthly interest rate)
- 36 into B3

Your results should agree with the worksheet shown in Figure 6.3.

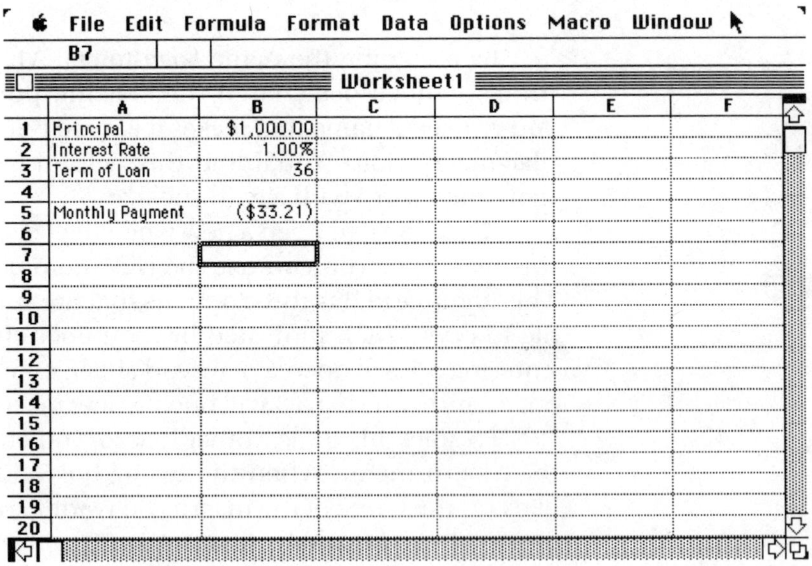

Figure 6.3 Results of Loan macro

When you used this macro, the NEW command in cell A2 on the macro sheet opened a new worksheet. Cell A1 on the worksheet was selected by the SELECT command in A2, and the label *Principal* was entered by the FORMULA command in A3.

In a similar manner, the commands in cells A5 through A10 selected various cells on the worksheet and entered the appropriate lables.

Next, the commands in cells A12 through A17 on the macro sheet selected cells B1, B2, and B3 on the worksheet and established the desired number formatting.

After that, the commands in A19, A20, and A21 on the macro sheet selected cell B5 on the worksheet, entered the formula, and established the number format.

Finally, the RETURN command in A22 on the macro sheet ended the macro, returning control back to the keyboard.

This macro contains only five commands: NEW, SELECT, FORMULA, FORMAT.NUMBER, and RETURN. From these basic commands, you were able to create a macro that accomplished a meaningful task. Further, you can use it any time by simply executing it.

Data Movement and Column Widths

Once you understand how these basic blocks are used, you can begin to explore alternative methods of entering data into specific cells via the clipboard or through cell references. Both of these useful methods are used too infrequently, which means that your tools are being used inefficiently.

Suppose you needed a template capable of determining not only the monthly payment, but the total amount you still owe, and how much you've paid. You can do this by building onto the basic commands you've just used.

Close both the macro and the worksheet without saving either one, then open a new macro sheet and enter the information shown in Figure 6.4.

	A	B	C
1	*Loan Information Template*	*Text Constants*	*Numeric Constants*
2	=SELECT(!A1)	No. of Payments Made	20
3	=FORMULA("Amount of Principal")	Total Amount Paid	
4	=SELECT(!A2)	Total Amount of Loan	
5	=FORMULA("Monthly Interest Rate")	No. Remaining Payments	
6	=SELECT(!A3)	Total Amount Remaining	
7	=FORMULA("Term of Loan in Months")		
8	=SELECT(,"R[2]C")		
9	=FORMULA("Monthly Payment")		
10	=SELECT(,"R[2]C")		
11	=FORMULA(B2)		
12	=SELECT(,"R[1]C")		
13	=FORMULA(B3)		
14	=SELECT(,"RC[2]")		
15	=FORMULA(B6)		
16	=SELECT(,"R[-1]C")		
17	=FORMULA(B5)		
18	=SELECT(,"R[-2]C")		
19	=FORMULA(B4)		
20	*Set Column Widths, Format Cells*		
21	=SELECT(!A:A)		
22	=COLUMN.WIDTH(20)		
23	=SELECT(!C:C)		
24	=COLUMN.WIDTH(C2)		
25	=SELECT(!B1)		
26	=FORMAT.NUMBER("$#,###.00 ;($#,###.00)")		
27	=SELECT(!B2)		
28	=FORMAT.NUMBER("##.00%")		
29	=SELECT(!B5:D5)		
30	=FORMAT.NUMBER("$#,###.00 ;($#,###.00)")		
31	=SELECT(!B8:D8)		
32	=FORMAT.NUMBER("$#,###.00 ;($#,###.00)")		
33	*Establish Formulas*		
34	=SELECT(!B5)		
35	=FORMULA("=IF(R3C2<=0,0,PMT(R2C2,R3C2,R1C2)")		
36	=SELECT(!D5)		
37	=FORMULA("=IF(R3C2<=0,0,R3C2*R5C2)")		
38	=SELECT(!D7)		
39	=FORMULA("=R3C2-R7C2")		
40	=SELECT(!D8)		
41	=FORMULA("=R[-1]C*R[-3]C[-2]")		
42	=SELECT(!B8)		
43	=FORMULA("=R[-1]C*R[-3]C")		
44	=SELECT(!A1)		
45	=RETURN()		

Figure 6.4 Revised Loan Information macro

The information in cells A1 through A7 uses the SELECT and FORMULA commands to enter the basic information in cells A1 through A3 of the worksheet. These you should be familiar with.

In cell A8, however, notice the address that appears within the parentheses. This form of relative RC addressing permits a range of cells to be selected with one particular cell designated as the active cell. Normally, the command would appear as

$$= SELECT(R1C1:R5C1,R5C1)$$

which would select the cell range A1:A5, with cell A5 as the active cell.

Here, the selection of a cell range has been omitted (nothing appears before the comma). As a result, the command selects the cell that is two rows below the last cell selected in the same column. This is caused by the absence of a number following the "C" in the command.

The **FORMULA** command in A9 on the macro sheet enters the text *Monthly Payment* into the currently selected cell on the worksheet; then A9 is followed by a command that is identical to the one in A8. Thus, by using relative RC-style addressing, you can copy the formula in A8 and paste it into A10.

In cell A11, the **FORMULA** command uses a cell reference as the source to enter the text into the worksheet. The absence of the exclamation mark designates cell B2 *on the macro sheet* as the source of the data to be entered into the active cell on the worksheet. This method allows you to store specific information as well as commands on the macro sheet that you are using to construct your worksheet.

The commands entered into cells A12 through A19 use a combination of relative RC addressing and macro sheet references to select and enter data on the next four cells of the worksheet with only one variation: a minus symbol precedes the row designator in the commands in cells A16 and A18. The command in cell A16 selects a cell one row before the active cell, and the command in cell A18 selects a cell two rows before the active cell. For example, if the active cell on the worksheet is B7, then the command in A16 on the macro sheet would cause cell B6 on the worksheet to be selected, since it is one row up.

In cell A21, the **SELECT** command is used to select an entire column on the worksheet; cell A21 is followed by the command that sets the width of the column selected.

The COLUMN.WIDTH command (be sure to observe the period) is shown here in its simplest form. In this variation of the command, the number in the parentheses specifies the desired column width and will widen column A to 20 characters.

Cell A23 again uses the SELECT command to select an entire column (C in this case); it is followed by a variation of the COLUMN.WIDTH command in A24. The COLUMN.WIDTH command uses the value located in cell C2 of the macro sheet as the width specification for the column.

The commands in A25, A26, A27, and A28 select cells B1 and B2 on the worksheet and establish numeric formats to display the cell contents as dollars and percentages respectively.

In A29, three cells (B5 through D5) are selected and formatted as dollars by the FORMAT.NUMBER command in A30. Selecting multiple cells and formatting all at once is one option you should keep in mind, since it can significantly reduce the number of commands required in your macros.

Notice that the data in cell C5 of the worksheet will be the text entry *Total Amount of Loan*. Even though a numeric format has been established for this cell, the text will still be properly formatted since numeric formats do not affect text.

The commands that appear in cells A31 and A32 also use the multiple-cell selection procedure to select and format cells B8 through D8 of the worksheet.

The command in A34 on the macro sheet selects cell B5 of the worksheet and enters a compound command. The compound command first checks the value in cell B3 on the worksheet to see if the value in B3 is less than or equal to zero. If so, the formula will display a zero. Otherwise, the PMT function is used to calculate the monthly payment. This prevents the #DIV/0! error value from appearing in cell B5 of the worksheet if no entry has been made in cell B3 of the worksheet, or if cells B1, B2, and B3 do not contain any entries.

The SELECT command in A36 selects cell D5 on the worksheet, and a compound command is entered into D5 by the FORMULA command in A37 of the worksheet. This formula compares the value in B3 of the worksheet to a value of zero. If it's less than or equal to zero, a zero is displayed in the cell. Otherwise, the total amount of the loan is computed by multiplying the total number of months (assuming one payment per month) by the monthly payment amount found in B5 of the worksheet.

The commands in A38 and A39 of the macro enter a formula into D7 of the worksheet that subtracts the number of payments made in cell B7 from the total number of months in cell B3. This computes the total number of payments remaining.

The value in D7 is multiplied by the value in cell B5 to compute the total amount of the loan remaining to be paid in monthly installments.

Similarly, the commands in A42 and A43 determine the total amount that has already been paid in monthly installments, which is entered into cell B8 of the worksheet.

Finally, the SELECT command in A44 of the macro sheet selects cell A1 to help prevent accidental destruction of the formulas (more on this subject a bit later), and the macro is ended by the RETURN command in A45.

Using the Loan Info Macro

To use this macro, select cell A1 and assign the name *Loan Info* to it, being sure to designate it as a Command Macro. Next, save the macro with any name you desire, then open a new worksheet.

After making sure the worksheet is active (click anywhere on it or choose its name via the Window menu), choose the Run option of the Macro menu, click Loan Info, and watch your worksheet being constructed.

When it's finished, enter the amount to be borrowed into cell B1, the monthly interest rate expressed as a decimal into B2, and the number of months you'll be paying on the loan into B3.

The worksheet will calculate all figures for the remaining cells except for cell B7. By entering the total number of payments that have been made on the loan, the figures in cells B8, D7, and D8 will be computed and displayed.

Caution

While this type of macro works quite well, it does contain a potentially dangerous situation. If the macro is executed when the macro sheet is still active, it will create the template *on the macro sheet* and, in so doing, will destroy the commands and data found in cells A1 through D8.

To prevent this situation, you can use the macro to create a new worksheet each time it's executed by inserting the NEW command into cell A2. After saving this macro, click on the macro sheet and then execute it.

To retrieve your original, close this macro *without* saving any changes and then reopen it.

After your test, modify the macro so it will open a new worksheet each time it's executed by selecting cell A2 of the macro, choosing the insert command from the Edit menu and making the entry shown below.

$$= NEW(1)$$

After making this modification, save the macro so the modification will not have to be made again.

Now when the macro is executed, a new worksheet will be opened, which is immediately designated as the active document on your desktop. This guarantees you'll never have to worry about destroying your macro.

Loops, Subroutines, and Dialog

Once you've mastered the basic commands used in macros, it's time to gain an in-depth understanding of program loops, subroutines, and dialog boxes. These are the elements you will use to make your macros more compact, faster, and easier to use.

You'll create program loops consisting of only four or five commands to perform the repetitive functions that would otherwise require 15, 20, or 25 commands. Program loops increase the speed of your macros.

Instead of writing the same procedure time after time at various locations, you'll write one subroutine that will be accessed by several different portions of your macro, thus reducing the size of your macros and making them easier to understand and modify.

You'll use the three different types of dialog boxes — Alert, Caution, and Note — to communicate with the user, making your macros easier to use.

Conditional Loops

In other programming languages, there are several different types of procedures that are known as *program loops*. These are nothing more than a repetitive execution of the same commands until a specified condition is met. As such, they can be called "conditional loops," since their operation is based on whether a particular requirement or condition is met. A typical example is entering a series of checks: the same commands are executed over and over (the loop) until another action is to be performed (the condition).

Open a new macro sheet and enter the information shown in Figure 6.5, which will execute the same two commands ten times.

	A
1	Loop1
2	=SELECT(!B1)
3	=FORMULA(!B1+1)
4	=IF(!B1<10,GOTO(A2),GOTO(A5))
5	=RETURN()
6	

Figure 6.5 Conditional loop in a macro

After entering the information, choose the Define Name option of the Formula menu and assign the name *Loop1* to cell A1 on the macro sheet, making sure you designate it as a command macro.

The macro begins by selecting cell B1 on the currently active worksheet, the result of the SELECT command in A2. Next, the FORMULA command in A3 takes whatever value is in cell B1 on the worksheet, adds one to it, and places the new value back into B1.

The IF command in cell A4 is the key decision maker in this loop. It compares the value currently in cell B1 of the worksheet to see if the value in B1 is less than ten. If it is less than ten, the sequence of execution is altered by the command GOTO(A2), and the macro resumes execution with cell A2 on the macro sheet.

If the value in B1 on the worksheet is equal to or greater than ten, then the second GOTO command will be executed, causing a branch to cell A5.

Thus, the commands in cells A2, A3, and A4 on the macro sheet will be executed a total of ten times before the RETURN command in A5 is executed once.

Open a new worksheet, use the Run option of the Macro menu to execute the macro named Loop1, and view the results.

One Step at a Time

Although you can see the numbers in B1 of the worksheet changing, you may find it difficult to relate the actions that are occurring to the commands that are causing them. Excel includes a handy little option that lets you slow things down and monitor each command and its results as the macro executes them.

To see how this option works, select cell A2 on the macro sheet, insert a cell, and enter the command shown below.

= STEP()

When you execute the macro with this command installed, a dialog box like the one shown in Figure 6.6 will appear on your monitor offering three options: Step, Halt, and Continue.

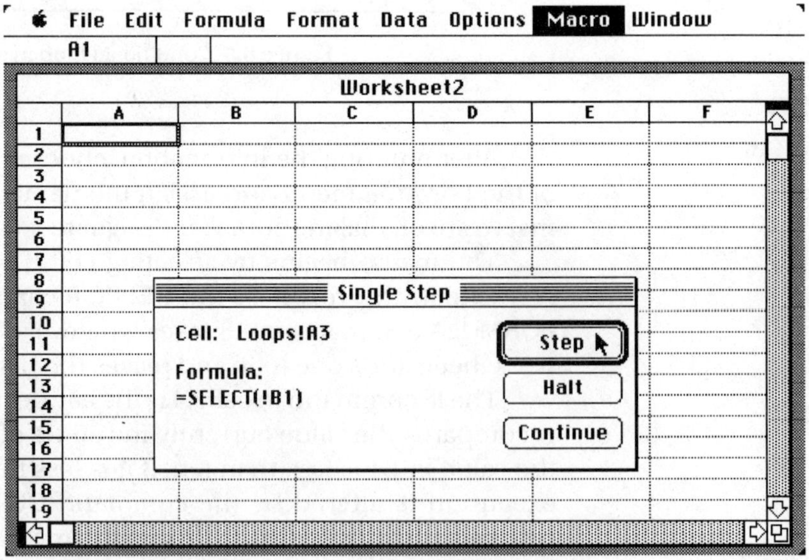

Figure 6.6 Results of the STEP command

Choosing the Step option will execute the command currently shown in the dialog box; the Halt option will stop the macro from executing; the Continue option will cause the macro to resume normal execution.

You may want to insert this command temporarily in every macro you write to verify that it operates correctly. Once you're confident that the macro operates correctly, simply delete the command.

Counters

There may be times when you want to perform a particular operation repetitively, but you do not want to use a value on the worksheet to control the loop. In such instances, you can establish a *counter* in a cell on the macro sheet to keep track of the number of times your loop has been executed. This method is used in the macro named Loop2, which is shown in Figure 6.7.

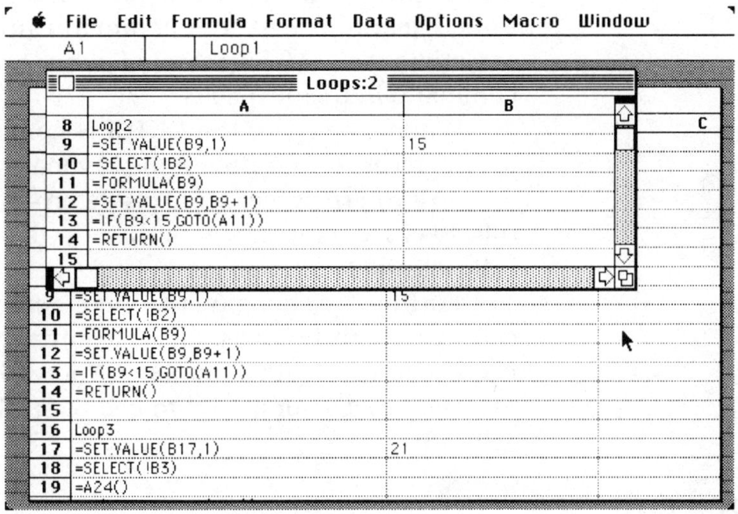

Figure 6.7 Loop2 macro, using a counter

Enter this macro on the same macro sheet that contains the macro named Loop1. After entering the information, choose the Define Name option of the Formula menu and assign the name Loop2 to cell A8, being sure to indicate that it's a command macro.

Notice the command in cell A9. This command, SET.VALUE, is used to establish and alter values on the macro sheet without disturbing the currently selected cell on the worksheet. As such, the first time it is executed, it will place a value of one into cell B9 on the macro sheet.

The command in A10 selects cell B2 on the worksheet. The FORMULA command in A11 places the current value in B9 of the macro sheet into the currently selected cell on the worksheet.

The SET.VALUE command in A12 is again used to set the value in B9 on the macro sheet. You'll notice that this time the cell address appears twice: once before the comma, to designate the cell where the value will be placed, and once after the comma, to designate the value that should be incremented by one.

Cell A13 uses a modified version of the IF command to control the execution of this loop. It first compares the value in cell B9 on the macro sheet to 15. If the value in B9 is 15 or less, the GOTO command causes a branch back to cell A11. If the value in B9 is 15 or greater, the GOTO command will not be executed, causing the macro to continue execution with the command in cell A14. (This method is sometimes called *falling through*, since execution *falls through* to the command in the next cell.)

When executed, the RETURN command in A14 will end the macro, returning control to the keyboard.

So if you're processing a predetermined number of items — payroll checks for employees, perhaps — this type of loop will automatically terminate after all your checks have been processed.

Further, by changing the increment value in cell A12, this loop can increment by twos, fours, twenties, or any other number you need — even negative numbers. You will, however, have to change the value that's compared to cell B9 in the IF command located in cell A13.

Subroutines

A subroutine is similar to a micro-macro. It is a specific series of commands that is used by several different parts of your macro, performing the same function whenever needed.

For example, many macros ask a question like "Is this correct (Y/N)," obtain the user's reply, then check the reply for correctness at several different points. Or perhaps you need to increment a particular value every time the user performs a certain task — such as automatically incrementing a check number.

If you use a subroutine for these types of functions, you'll only need to write the routine once instead of several times. Then, whenever you need the function, you can access the subroutine.

Using the same macro sheet that now contains the macros named Loop1 and Loop2, enter the information shown in Figure 6.8 into cells A16 through A26 of the macro sheet.

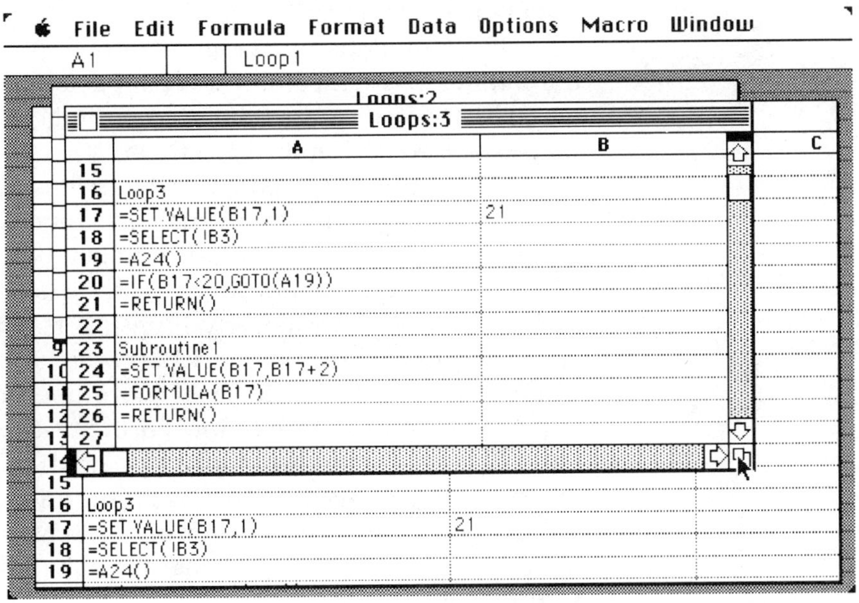

Figure 6.8 Loop3 macro, using a subroutine

Next, assign the name *Loop3* to cell A16, designating it as a command macro. You may also want to insert the STEP command into cell A17 temporarily to allow slower execution.

Except for cell addresses, the SET.VALUE and SELECT commands in cells A17 and A18 of Loop3 are identical to those used in the macro named Loop2. They establish the initial value of B17 on the macro sheet and select B3 on the worksheet.

In cell A19, however, you'll find nothing more than a cell address followed by a set of parentheses. This procedure, used to execute a subroutine, is more commonly known as *calling* a subroutine. When Excel encounters this command, it will temporarily transfer execution of the macro to the beginning of the subroutine located in cell A24 of the macro sheet.

The commands in A24 and A25 operate exactly the same way the commands in A11 and A12 of Loop2 do: they increment the value found in B17 of the macro sheet, then duplicate that value in the currently selected cell on the worksheet.

When the RETURN command in A26 is executed, it terminates operation of the subroutine, causing a branch back to cell A20 — the cell immediately after the one that called the subroutine.

If you used this subroutine in the Loan Info macro (possibly within a loop), the relatively long FORMAT.NUMBER commands appearing in cells A26, A30, and A32 could have been replaced with a single subroutine, resulting in more compact macro code that requires less development time. Further, since a subroutine is written only once, the possibility of a typographical error entering one of the three statements that it replaces is reduced by about 66 percent.

You can see several examples of how subroutines are used in actual applications by taking a sneak preview of the macro in Figure 7.3 in Chapter 7.

Effective Dialog

Most integrated applications that use macros incorporate a method to communicate with the user. Excel provides three different commands to pass information to the user and one to obtain the user's reply. The three commands that pass information to the user are collectively known as "Alert dialog," and the command to obtain data from the user is known as "Input dialog."

Individually, the three Alert commands (sometimes called "dialog boxes") are Caution, Note, and Stop Alerts, and are referred to by the numbers 1, 2, and 3, respectively. They are shown in Figure 6.9.

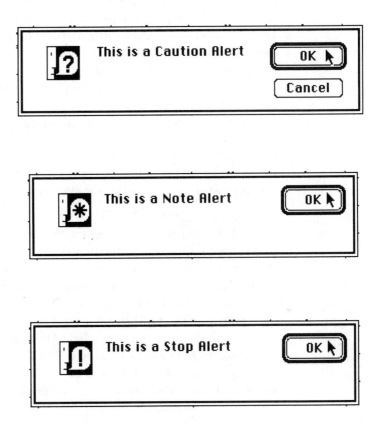

Figure 6.9 Caution, Note, and Stop Alerts

For example, a Caution Alert command might read:

$$= ALERT(\text{"Are you sure?"},1)$$

The phrase enclosed in quotation marks will be displayed on the monitor, while the 1 signifies this is a Caution Alert. To change this command to a Note Alert, you would change the 1 to a 2.

A Caution Alert is used when you want to verify a particular operation the user is about to perform or has just performed; a Note Alert is used when you want to inform the user of something; a Stop Alert is used when you want to alert the user to a potentially hazardous operation, such as deleting a file.

Both Alert and Input dialog boxes can include text — either enclosed within quotation marks or by using a cell reference — to be displayed and can temporarily halt macro execution until the user is ready to proceed.

The Note box, for example, can be incorporated into the Loop1 macro to focus the user's attention. Select cell A4, insert a blank cell, and enter the command shown below.

= ALERT("The value in B1 is now "&!B1,2)

When the macro is executed, this command will join the phrase *The value in B1 is now* with the value currently in cell B1 (caused by the &!B1 in the command) of the worksheet. Every time the number in cell B1 on the worksheet changes, the new value will be displayed, as shown in Figure 6.10.

This type of alert box offers the user only one selection, the OK button. When the user either clicks OK or presses the Return key, the Alert box returns a logical value of TRUE.

The Note Alert is identical to the Stop Alert, except for the icon displayed. The Note box uses an asterisk as its icon, while the Stop box adds more emphasis by using the exclamation mark as its icon.

The Caution box uses the question mark as its icon and provides the user with two options: clicking either an OK or the Cancel button. If the user clicks OK, the results returned will be a logical TRUE. If the Cancel button is clicked, the results will be a logical FALSE.

	A	B
1	Loop1	
2	=STEP()	
3	=SELECT(!B1)	
4	=ALERT("The value in B1 is now "&!B1,2)	
5	=FORMULA(!B1+1)	
6	=IF(!B1<10,GOTO(A3),GOTO(A7))	
7	=RETURN()	
8		
9	Loop2	15
10	=SET.VALUE(B9,1)	
11	=SELECT(!B2)	
12	=FORMULA(B9)	
13	=SET.VALUE(B9,B9+1)	
14	=IF(B9<15,GOTO(A12))	
15	=RETURN()	
16		
17	Loop3	0
18	=SET.VALUE(B17,1)	
19	=SELECT(!B3)	
20	=A25()	
21	=IF(B17<20,GOTO(A20))	
22	=RETURN()	
23		
24	Subroutine1	
25	=SET.VALUE(B17,B17+2)	
26	=FORMULA(B17)	
27	=RETURN()	

Figure 6.10 Loop1 macro

Unlike the Alert boxes, which provide only limited interaction with the user, the Input dialog box — shown in Figure 6.11 — gives you almost unlimited interaction. You can display messages and request specific replies in the form of logical values, numbers, text, or even cell references.

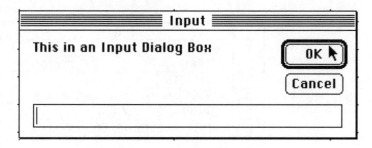

Figure 6.11 Input dialog box

The Input dialog has three parameters associated with it, *prompt*, *type*, and *title*. The prompt is the phrase that will be displayed on the monitor; type is a number specifying the acceptable types of response by the user; and title is an optional phrase that will be inserted into the title bar of the dialog box. Both the prompt and the title can be either cell references or enclosed within quotation marks.

The type specification can be one of seven different values, which determine exactly what the Input dialog box will accept. These are:

0 Formula. Any formula normally accepted by Excel, such as (2 + 5)*3 or (B7 + G3)*(H2 + A5)/4.

1 Number. Any number usable in a math formula.

2 Text. Any phrase or number that is to be treated as text for non-numerical operations.

4 Logical. Either True or False.

8 Reference. Any cell reference, such as $B$3, Budget!C5, Checks!Written, or B2:G7.

16 Error value. Any of Excel's error values such as #N/A, #DIV/0!, etc.

64 Array. Any array value.

So, a command reading

= INPUT("Enter Check Amount",1,B5)

would display the phrase *Enter Check Amount* in the dialog box, would accept only numbers in response (specified by the "1"), and would display the contents of cell B5 in the title bar.

You can also specify that more than one type of input is acceptable from the user. To do this, decide which types of response you'll allow, then sum their values and use that number as your specification.

For example, if you used the number 3 instead of 1 in the Input box requesting the check amount, Excel would accept either a number or text as a valid response. A number is indicated by a value of 1, and text is indicated by a value of 2. Adding them both together — 1 + 2 — provides the new specification of 3.

Summary

In this chapter, you learned how to establish and control program loops through the use of counters and how to create subroutines. You learned the advantages that subroutines provide and the different types of dialog that can make your applications easier to use.

By establishing dialog boxes as subroutines and incorporating controlling loops into your macros, you will have compact macros that are easy to use, require less memory, and execute much faster.

In the next chapter, you'll use all of these tools to create a fully integrated application. It will show you only a few of the many possible combinations that you can use to make your applications more effective.

CHAPTER

Your Personal Accounting System

In this chapter, you'll use all the information you've learned in earlier sections to create an application that makes extensive use of macros. You'll learn how to manipulate the display options to change a common worksheet so that it looks like an applications menu and how to make effective use of dialog boxes, loops, and subroutines.

You'll create all of the worksheets and macros you need to maintain your personal accounting system, the check register, which is perhaps the most common financial application of all.

In Chapter 8, you'll expand the application to provide printed reports by using macros to design the reports, summarize the data, and do the actual printing.

Creating the Worksheets

The first worksheet you'll create, named CR.Data, is a slightly modified version of what you'll find in the check register that accompanies most check books. It contains columns for the check number, the date of transaction, a memorandum, a category, and a transaction amount.

All of these are used exactly the same way their manual counterparts are, with the exception of the category and amount entries. With the category entry, you'll assign a specific code or account number to each transaction; the code or number will be used later to search and summarize the data by group. For example, you might decide to assign all medical payments to a category named Med. You can then obtain the entire total of all medical payments with a DSUM command.

To create the worksheet, open a new worksheet via the File menu and make the entries shown below.

Cell	Entry	Width	Format
A1	Check#	8	Bold/Center
B1	Date	12	Bold/Center
C1	Memorandum	23	Bold/Center
D1	Category	8	Bold/Center
E1	Amount	12	Bold/Center

It isn't necessary to establish data formats for the columns, since the macro you'll create will take care of that.

Notice that this worksheet does not contain separate columns for checks and deposits. Both of these entries are made in colum E, (the Amount column); this technique is based on the premise that deposits are positive numbers, since they increase the balance, and checks are negative numbers that decrease the balance.

After creating the worksheet, save it with the name *CR.Data*, making sure that you include the period in the file name.

Next, you can take advantage of Excel's many display and formatting options to create a menu that will be used to access the various functions offered by the macro.

Open another worksheet and make the entries shown below in the cells indicated, being sure to observe the formatting options. You'll note that columns A and E are adjusted to a width of 15 characters, even though there are no entries in either column.

Cell	Entry
C1	Personal Accounting System
C2	Version 1.0
C4	(If the menu is obscured, move dialog box by dragging its title bar.)
C6	1 — Make a Deposit
C7	2 — Write a Check
C8	3 — Print Check Register
C9	4 — Print Summary Report
C10	5 — View Current Status
C11	6 — Quit

Column Widths and Formats

Cell	Width	Format	Alignment
A1	15	N/A	
C1	10	Bold	Center
C2	N/A	N/A	Center
C4	N/A	Italic	Center
C6:C11	N/A	N/A	Left

After entering and formatting the data, choose the Display option of the Options menu and make certain that none of the boxes is checked. Double-click the title bar of the worksheet to cause it to occupy the full space of your monitor, then select cell C16. Upon completion, your worksheet should resemble the one shown in Figure 7.1. If so, save the worksheet with the name CR.Menu.

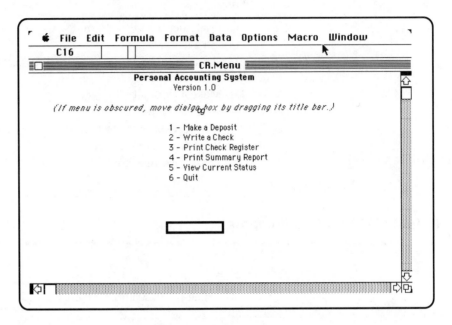

Figure 7.1 CR.Menu worksheet

CR.Macro

The CR.Macro consists of several individual macros and includes several subroutines. Additionally, several areas of the worksheet have been set aside to hold various data elements used to keep track of the number of entries made on the CR.Data worksheet, pass information to the user, and obtain data from the user.

Due to the size and complexity of this macro, each of the individual macros and their associated components will be examined and tested separately. This will make it easier for you to understand each function that the macro performs.

Additionally, each routine and segment is identified with a comment displayed in bold italic type that associates it with a particular macro or function.

The Menu

The first macro, shown in Figure 7.2, is identified by the word *Menu* in cell A1. It serves not only as the initial starting point for the application, but it initializes all variables, opens all worksheets, determines menu selections, and ends the macro as well.

	A	B
1	*Menu*	*General Data*
2	=MESSAGE(TRUE,B4)	Verify Data
3	=Init.Vars()	Is the information shown correct (Y=Yes; N=No)?
4	=Open.Wks()	Initializing All Functions, Please Wait....
5	=MESSAGE(TRUE,B13)	
6	=ACTIVATE("CR.Menu")	*Temporary Worksheet File Names*
7	=INPUT(B14,7,B13)	Dep.Temp
8	=IF(A7=FALSE,GOTO(A28))	Chk.Temp
9	=SET.VALUE(A7,VALUE(A7))	Rpt.Temp
10	=IF(OR(A7<1,A7>6),Error1(),GOTO(A12))	Sum.Temp
11	=GOTO(A7)	
12	=IF(A7=1,Deposit())	*Menu Data*
13	=IF(A7=2,Check())	Transaction Selection
14	=IF(A7=3,Register())	Enter your selection by number.
15	=IF(A7=4,Summary())	Your selection must be a number between 1 and 6.
16	=IF(A7=5,Status())	
17	=IF(A7=6,GOTO(A19))	*Deposit Data*
18	=GOTO(A5)	Enter date of deposit (Example: MM/DD/YY)
19	=Clean.Up()	Enter memoranda for deposit
20	=Init.Vars()	Enter category of deposit
21	=ACTIVATE("CR.Data")	Enter deposit amount (No $ symbol; No commas)
22	=SAVE()	Enter another deposit (Y=Yes; N=No)?
23	=CLOSE()	
24	=ACTIVATE("CR.Menu")	*Check Data*
25	=CLOSE()	Enter check number
26	=ACTIVATE("CR.Macro")	Enter date of check (Example: MM/DD/YY)
27	=SAVE()	Enter memoranda for check
28	=RETURN()	Enter category of check
29		Enter check amount (No $ symbol; No commas)
30	*Error1*	Enter another check (Y=Yes; N=No)?
31	=ALERT(B15,3)	
32	=RETURN()	*Number of entries on CR.Data Worksheet*
33		0
34		
35		
36		
37		

Figure 7.2 Menu macro

After entering this part of the CR.Macro, assign the name *Start* to cell A1 with the Define Name option of the Formula menu, even though the cell contains the word *Menu*.

Assigning a different name to this cell means that when the Run option of the Macro menu is chosen, the phrase in the dialog box will be CR.Macro!Start. This helps your user understand what this particular selection, if it is chosen, will do — it will start the CR.Macro. You've also maintained the legibility of the macro listing by using the word *Menu* in the cell, since it identifies the function of commands that follow it.

If the logical value within the parentheses is TRUE, the command in cell A2 displays a message immediately below the Excel's menu bar. The text for the message, specified by the cell reference B4, is the phrase *Menu Data*.

The commands in cells A3 and A4 call two subroutines in sequence. Instead of calling the subroutines with a cell reference like =A29(), each subroutine has been assigned a name. Using the names *Init.Vars* and *Open.Wks* (located in cells A34 and A41) makes it easy to understand the purpose of each subroutine. These particular subroutines will be examined individually a bit later.

The MESSAGE command in A5 replaces the message currently displayed with the phrase in B13, to provide the user with information concerning the current operation.

In A6, the ACTIVATE command is used to make the CR.Menu worksheet active; putting ACTIVATE in a macro is the same as clicking the worksheet with the mouse. The quotation marks are required at all times, unless a cell reference is used instead of the actual name.

Next, the INPUT command in A7 requests the user to enter a number designating one of the menu options. The prompt phrase is obtained from cell B14 on the macro sheet, and the phrase for the title bar is obtained from cell B13. This results in the display shown in Figure 7.3.

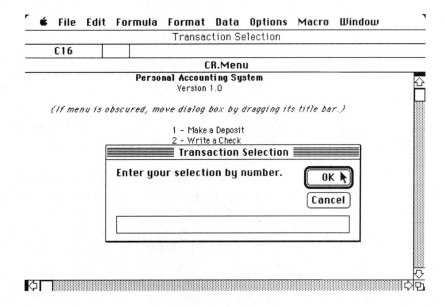

Figure 7.3 CR.Macro menu display

The value of 7 used in the INPUT command in cell A7 specifies that the input made by the user can be a logical value, some text, a formula, or a number. It is obtained by adding the values shown in the *Excel User's Guide* for each data type: $0 + 1 + 2 + 4 = 7$.

The IF command in cell A8 checks to see if the value entered by the user was the logical value FALSE; if the value is false, Excel immediately branches to cell A28. This will cause the macro to end, since A28 contains a RETURN command. Note that "entering a logical value" does not mean simply clicking OK or Cancel, but actually entering the word FALSE as your response and then choosing OK.

Next, the user's response must be converted into a numeric value. In cell A9, the SET.VALUE command converts the text representation of the number entered by the user (assuming that a number was entered) into a numeric value. This command can be used to place a particular value in any cell by first supplying the cell reference (A7 in this case) and the value to be entered into the cell. Here the embedded VALUE command is used to convert the text entry in A7 into a number, which is then placed back into the same cell.

You should keep in mind that the SET.VALUE command can be used to produce any value in a cell (text, number, logical, etc.), but it can be used only with cells on a macro sheet and will not work on cells located on a worksheet.

The value in A7 is then checked to determine if the user chose one of the available menu selections. In cell A10, a compound command consisting of the OR and IF functions is used to see if the value currently in A7 is less than one or greater than six. If so, the user has made an invalid selection and the subroutine named *Error1* will be called. Otherwise, the GOTO command is executed to transfer execution to cell A12.

If Error1 was called, execution will resume with the command in cell A11, a procedure known as an unconditional branch. In this form, the GOTO command will always alter the sequence of execution, transferring control back to the command located in cell A7 — the start of the input routine. This ensures the integrity of the menu selection process by obtaining another selection from the user any time an invalid selection is made.

The IF commands in cells A12 through A17 perform a series of comparisons to determine exactly which selection the user made and then to branch to the appropriate function. Notice that if selections one through five are chosen, a named subroutine will be executed. If selection number six is chosen, the macro uses a GOTO command to branch to the command in A19.

When Excel returns from one of the subroutines, all of the following comparisons caused by the remaining IF commands will fail, since the value in A7 has not been changed. As a result, the GOTO command in A18 will be executed, transferring execution back to cell A5. This causes the menu to be displayed, and the selection process is again initiated.

When the user finally chooses selection number six, several actions occur. The commands in cells A19 and A20 are executed, calling two subroutines. One will close and delete any temporary worksheets that were created, and the other will reset all program variables.

The ACTIVATE command in A21 then activates the CR.Data worksheet, saves it with the SAVE command in A22, and then closes the CR.Data worksheet with the CLOSE command in A23.

Next, the ACTIVATE and SAVE commands in cells A26 and A27 will activate the CR.Macro sheet and save its present state, to prevent Excel from asking the user if worksheet changes should be saved before closing. Execution then proceeds to the RETURN command in A28, which ends the macro.

The commands in cells A30, A31, and A32 form a simple subroutine that will use a Stop Alert to display the phrase contained in cell B15. This phrase informs the user that a selection between one and six must be made. When the user clicks the OK button, the RETURN command will end the subroutine, returning control to the cell immediately following the cell that called it.

Thus, if the user makes an invalid selection, the dialog box shown in Figure 7.4 provides a gentle reminder about the selections allowed.

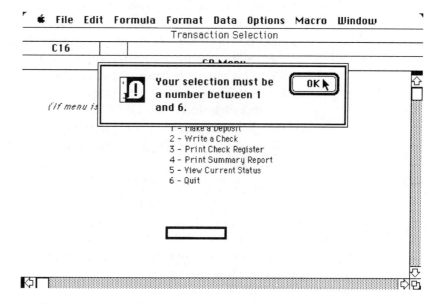

Figure 7.4 Error message display

The subroutine that occupies cells A38 through A43 is used to establish four named variables: *Dep*, which indicates the presence of a temporary worksheet used for deposits; *Chk*, which indicates a temporary worksheet used for writing checks; *Rpt* and *Sum*, also temporary worksheets used for compiling reports. Containing a logical value, either TRUE or FALSE, each of the four variables is used by other portions of the macro to determine if a particular temporary worksheet has been created.

The SET.NAME commands simulate using the Define Name or Create Name menu options, in that they establish named references, which are assigned the logical value of FALSE. You can assign any value with the SET.NAME command — they can be text, numeric, or logical values, and so on — but, you must always enclose the names in quotation marks.

If you assign the name *Init.Vars* to this subroutine with the Define Name option, Excel will automatically adjust the address if the subroutine is moved. This ensures the integrity of your macro, since the subroutine is always referenced by its name.

The subroutine named *Open.Wks* is located in cells A45 through A50. This routine opens the worksheets named CR.Data and CR.Menu and sets their windows to full size.

This variation of the OPEN command will update any references to worksheets that are linked to the Cr.Data or CR.Menu worksheets (although none are). You can prevent this by using the second form of the command:

OPEN("CR.Data",FALSE)

The FULL command has two options, TRUE and FALSE, which correspond to double-clicking the title bar of a worksheet to change its size. If the TRUE option is used, the worksheet will occupy the entire video monitor. If the FALSE option is used, the worksheet will revert to its former size.

The next subroutine located in column A is the subroutine named *Clean.Up*. As its name implies, it performs clean-up operations before the macro ends by closing all open worksheets, deleting any nonessential temporary worksheets, and so on.

The Clean.Up subroutine sequentially checks each of the named definitions established by the Init.Vars subroutine. Any flag containing a logical value of TRUE indicates the presence of one of the temporary worksheets whose names appear in cells B7 through

B10. If the worksheet exists, it is activated by the ACTIVATE commands (cells A54, A58, A62, A66), saved and closed by calling the subroutine *Save.It* (cells A51, A55, A59, A63), and subsequently deleted with the FILE.DELETE commands appearing in cells A56, A60, A64, and A68.

The subroutine named *Save.It* , consisting of only three cells, saves and closes the active worksheet. Save.It has been placed in B38, B39, and B40 instead of column A to make it easier to present the macro listings in this book. You may prefer to place the routine in column A.

First, the SAVE command is used to save the currently active worksheet, followed by the CLOSE command to close the worksheet, and finally the RETURN command to end the subroutine.

If the worksheet were closed without first being saved, the familiar dialog box asking the user if the changes to the worksheet should be saved would appear. Since these are temporary worksheets that the user (theoretically) knows nothing about, the dialog box would only cause confusion.

Except for the number that appears in cell B33 and the Save.It subroutine, all of the information in column B consists of worksheet names and phrases used by the various routines in the macro. These have been grouped into units with the appropriate identification title shown in bold italic type.

The number in B33 is used to keep track of the number of entries that have been made to the CR.Data worksheet. Every time a deposit is made or a check is written, this value will be increased by one.

The portion of the CR.Macro that you've just created controls the overall operation by presenting the menu, determining selections, and calling the correct subroutine. Now, you'll create the subroutine that will let the user make deposits.

Making a Deposit

If the user has chosen selection one from the CR.Menu worksheet, the IF command in cell A12 calls the subroutine named *Deposit*, which occupies cells C1 through C34, as shown in Figure 7.5. Thus, it is not only possible to have more than one routine per column, you can also place them anywhere on the macro sheet *without* designating them as command macros. In fact, the only routine on this macro sheet designated as a command macro is the named reference *Start* , which appears in cell A1.

	C
1	*Deposit*
2	=IF(Dep=FALSE,Deposit.Wks())
3	=MESSAGE(TRUE,"Deposit Entry")
4	=ACTIVATE(B7)
5	=SELECT(!B1:B4)
6	=EDIT.DELETE(2)
7	=ALIGNMENT(2)
8	=SELECT(!B1)
9	=FORMULA(INPUT(B18,1,B17))
10	=FORMAT.NUMBER("mmmm d, yyyy")
11	=SELECT(!B2)
12	=FORMULA(INPUT(B19,2,B17))
13	=SELECT(!B3)
14	=FORMULA(INPUT(B20,2,B17))
15	=SELECT(!B4)
16	=FORMULA(INPUT(B21,1,B17))
17	=FORMAT.NUMBER("$#,###.00")
18	=SELECT(!B16)
19	=INPUT(B3,2,B2)
20	=IF(OR(C19="N",C19="n"),GOTO(C5))
21	=SET.NAME("Dcntr",0)
22	=ACTIVATE(B7)
23	=SELECT(OFFSET(!B1,Dcntr,0))
24	=COPY()
25	=ACTIVATE("CR.Data")
26	=SELECT(OFFSET(!B2,B33,Dcntr))
27	=PASTE()
28	=IF(Dcntr<3,SET.NAME("Dcntr",Dcntr+1),GOTO(C30))
29	=GOTO(C22)
30	=SET.VALUE(B33,B33+1)
31	=ACTIVATE(B7)
32	=INPUT(B22,2,B2)
33	=IF(OR(C32="Y",C32="y"),GOTO(C4),MESSAGE(FALSE))
34	=RETURN()
35	
36	
37	

Figure 7.5 Deposit macro

The IF command in C2 checks the value of the named definition *Dep* and, if it contains the value FALSE, calls the subroutine named *Deposit.Wks* to create the temporary worksheet that will be used to enter all deposits.

The MESSAGE command in C3 then displays the phrase *Deposit Entry* below the menu bar, and the temporary worksheet used for deposits is activated by the ACTIVATE command in C4.

To clear any data that might interfere with entering a deposit, cells B1 through B4 are selected and the EDIT.DELETE command is used to delete any information currently in those cells. This command is identical to the Delete option of the Edit menu, and uses the numeric value 2 to specify that the cells should be shifted up. Using a value of 1 would cause the cells to be shifted left, which could be used with equal success.

Since the four cells (B1:B4) are still selected, they can be formatted with the second option of the Alignment command which left justifies all data. As you'll see, left justifying the data provides a more visually appealing display.

Cell B1 on the temporary worksheet is selected in preparation for data entry by the command that is in cell C8. The actual data entry is performed by the compound command in C9, which enters the value obtained by the INPUT command directly into the currently selected cell.

Here, a value of 1 is used to specify that a numeric entry is required from the user. The prompt that will be displayed in the dialog box is obtained from cell B18 on the macro sheet. The title for the dialog box is taken from cell B17 on the macro sheet, as are the titles for all the deposit entry dialog boxes.

The FORMAT.NUMBER command is used in C10 to format the number as a date, and the SELECT command in C11 selects the next cell (B2) on the worksheet in preparation for the next entry.

In a similar manner, the commands in cells C12 through C16 obtain the data for the next three cells (Memorandum, Category, and Amount, respectively), the last of which is formatted by the FORMAT.NUMBER command in C17.

After all of the data has been entered for the deposit, the SELECT command in C18 then selects cell B16 on the worksheet. This will ensure that the active cell on the worksheet will be obscured when the next input box is displayed.

To verify the deposit data, the INPUT command in C19 uses the phrase located in B3 of the macro sheet and the title shown in B2 to ask the user if the information shown is correct. The letters "Y" and "y" will indicate a positive or "Yes" response, and "N" or "n" will indicate a negative or "No" response.

The entry made by the user is then checked by the compound IF command in C20 to see if the letter "N" has been entered in uppercase or lowercase. If so, a branch to cell C5 will delete the data currently shown and begin the entry process again. Any other entry is *assumed* to be a positive, or "Yes," response.

Next, the deposit data is transferred from the temporary worksheet to the CR.Data worksheet, which is accomplished by a program loop beginning with cell C21.

The SET.NAME command in C21 establishes the named reference (or variable) *Dcntr* with a value of zero. This variable will control the loop consisting of cells C22 through C29, which does the actual transfer.

After the variable has been established, the ACTIVATE command in C22 activates the worksheet whose name is shown in B7 of the macro sheet. This is the temporary deposit worksheet.

In C23, a new command called OFFSET is used in conjunction with the SELECT command to select a particular cell depending on the value of the variable *Dcntr*. The three parameters used with this command (*reference address, row offset, column offset*) establish B1 on the worksheet as the reference address; the row and column offset parameters are numbers that specify both the direction and the distance from the reference cell.

If a negative number is entered for the row offset, the result is to select a cell a certain number of rows above the reference address, while a positive number selects a cell below the reference address.

Similarly, a negative number for the column address indicates a cell to the left of the reference. A positive number indicates a cell to the right of the reference.

Since the variable Dcntr is used as the row offset and initially has a value of zero, cell B1 on the worksheet will be selected, since there is effectively no offset for either the row or column.

Now that the deposit data has been selected, the clipboard will be used to transfer the data from the temporary worksheet to the CR.Data worksheet.

The COPY command in C24 copies the contents of the current selection to the clipboard just as if you had chosen the Copy option of the Edit menu.

After the information has been copied to the clipboard, the ACTIVATE command in C25 is used to activate the CR.Data worksheet.

When the data is on the clipboard, the correct location on the CR.Data worksheet must be determined so that the data can be pasted into the CR.Data worksheet.

The OFFSET command is again used to select the correct cell on the CR.Data worksheet. In this instance, however, the reference cell is B2 instead of A2, since there is no check number associated with deposits.

Since the data must be positioned both horizontally and vertically, the row offset is taken from cell B33 on the macro sheet, which contains the total number of entries in the CR.Data worksheet, while the variable Dcntr is used as the column offset.

Since the variable Dcntr still contains a value of zero and the value in B33 is currently zero (assuming that this is the first entry), the cell selected on the CR.Data worksheet will be cell B2.

Thus, this procedure has selected cell B1 on the temporary worksheet, copied it to the clipboard, activated the CR.Data worksheet, and selected cell B2.

The PASTE command in cell C27 then pastes the data from the clipboard into the currently selected cell. As a result, the date of the deposit is transferred to the correct location on the CR.Data worksheet.

To transfer the remaining items, the IF command in C28 is used to compare the value of the variable Dcntr to see if it is less than three. If so, the SET.NAME command is executed, and the value of Dcntr is incremented by one in preparation for the next cell to be transferred from the temporary worksheet to the CR.Data worksheet.

The value of three is chosen since there are four items (Date, Memorandum, Category, and Amount) to be transferred. As Dcntr initially starts with a zero, the loop will repeat this process *four* times —zero, one, two, and three — and then will proceed to the command in C29.

If, on the other hand, Dcntr is equal to three, then the GOTO command is executed and the macro branches to cell C30.

The GOTO command in C29 is an unconditional branch and always transfers control to cell C22, the start of the loop.

The command in C30 is executed only after the entire deposit has been transferred to the CR.Data worksheet. Its purpose is to increment the value in the cell that contains the number of entries on the CR.Data worksheet (B33). Incrementing the value in the cell means that the offset command will always select the proper row.

After the deposit has been transferred and the number of entries on the CR.Data worksheet has been updated, the user is asked if another deposit is to be made. This is accomplished by the commands in C30 and C31. If there is another deposit to be made, the GOTO command in C33 causes a branch to C4, which will initiate the deposit routine again.

Otherwise, the MESSAGE command in C33 removes the message currently displayed below the menu bar. Since there are no more deposits to be entered, the RETURN command in C34 is executed, which ends the subroutine and returns control to cell A13.

Deposit.Wks Subroutine

The subroutine named *Deposit.Wks* (shown in Figure 7.6) occupies cells C38 through C58 and is used to create a temporary worksheet for entering all deposit information.

The commands in C39 through C47 open a new worksheet (C39), sequentially select cells A1 through A4 on the worksheet (C40, C42, C44, C46), and enter the labels that will be used to identify portions of the deposit (C41, C43, C45, C47).

Next, cells A1 through A4 are selected by the command in C48, the width of all columns is set to 12 by the COLUMN.WIDTH command in C49, and the Right option of the Alignment menu is specified by the command in C50.

	C
38	*Deposit.Wks*
39	=NEW(1)
40	=SELECT(!A1)
41	=FORMULA("Deposit Date: ")
42	=SELECT(!A2)
43	=FORMULA("Memoranda: ")
44	=SELECT(!A3)
45	=FORMULA("Category: ")
46	=SELECT(!A4)
47	=FORMULA("Amount: ")
48	=SELECT(!A1:A4)
49	=COLUMN.WIDTH(12)
50	=ALIGNMENT(4)
51	=STYLE(TRUE,FALSE)
52	=COLUMN.WIDTH(25,!B1)
53	=SELECT(!B1)
54	=SET.NAME("Dep",TRUE)
55	=DISPLAY(FALSE,FALSE,FALSE)
56	=FULL(TRUE)
57	=SAVE.AS(B7)
58	=RETURN()
59	
60	
61	
62	
63	
64	
65	
66	
67	
68	
69	

Figure 7.6 Deposit.Wks subroutine

In C51 the Bold option of the Style menu is selected because the first parameter specifies a logical value of TRUE, while the Italic option is set to off with the value FALSE.

A variation of the Column.Width command is used in C52 to set the width of column B to 25. This variation allows the width of any column to be adjusted *without* actually selecting the cell in the column.

After the column width has been set, the SELECT command in C53 selects cell B1 in preparation for data entry.

Once the worksheet has been created, the SET.NAME command in C54 changes the value of the variable *Dep* from FALSE to TRUE, indicating that the temporary worksheet is now created.

The worksheet display options are then set by the DISPLAY command in C55. The DISPLAY command turns off all row and column headings, gridlines, and so on, and sets the worksheet size to occupy the entire screen. Then the temporary worksheet is saved with the name that appears in cell B7 on the macro sheet.

The subroutine ends with the RETURN command that appears in cell C58.

Figure 7.7 shows a deposit entered into the temporary worksheet named *Dep.Temp*, and Figure 7.8 shows the same deposit after transfer to the CR.Data worksheet.

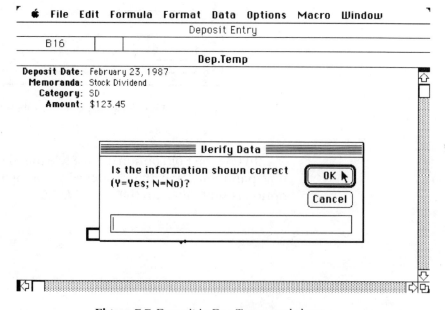

Figure 7.7 Deposit in Dep.Temp worksheet

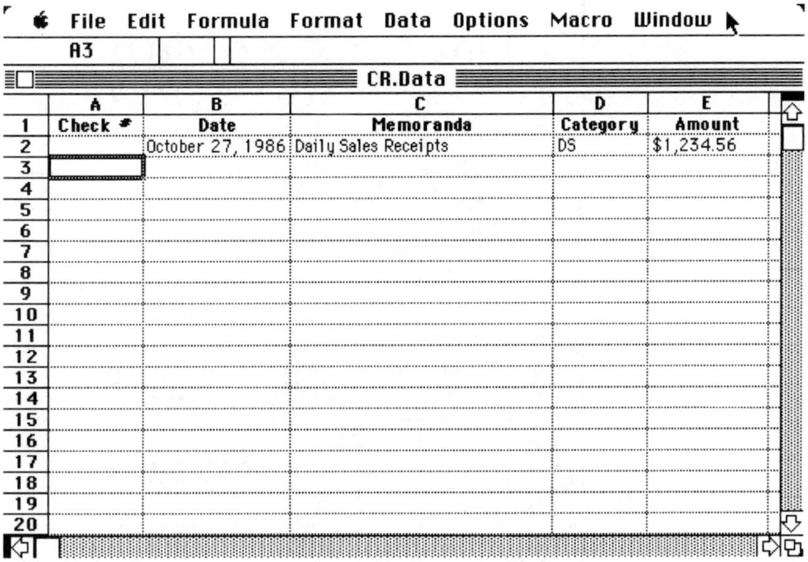

Figure 7.8 CR.Data worksheet containing deposit

Writing Checks

Now that you have the capability to enter and maintain all deposits, you must create the macros to maintain information about your checks.

When the user chooses selection 2 from the CR.Menu worksheet, the IF command A13 calls the subroutine named *Check*, shown in Figure 7.9.

	D
1	*Check*
2	=IF(Chk=FALSE,Check.Wks())
3	=MESSAGE(TRUE,"Check Entry")
4	=ACTIVATE(B8)
5	=SELECT(!B1:B5)
6	=EDIT.DELETE(2)
7	=ALIGNMENT(2)
8	=SELECT(!B1)
9	=FORMULA(INPUT(B25,2,B24))
10	=SELECT(!B2)
11	=FORMULA(INPUT(B26,1,B24))
12	=FORMAT.NUMBER("mmmm d, yyyy")
13	=SELECT(!B3)
14	=FORMULA(INPUT(B27,2,B24))
15	=SELECT(!B4)
16	=FORMULA(INPUT(B28,2,B24))
17	=SELECT(!B5)
18	=FORMULA(-INPUT(B29,1,B24))
19	=FORMAT.NUMBER("$#,###.00_,($#,###.00)")
20	=SELECT(!B16)
21	=INPUT(B3,2,B2)
22	=IF(OR(D21="N",D21="n"),GOTO(D5))
23	=ACTIVATE("CR.Data")
24	=SELECT(OFFSET(!A2,B33,0):OFFSET(!A2,B33,4))
25	=FORMULA.ARRAY("=TRANSPOSE(Chk.Temp!R1C2:R5C2)")
26	=SET.VALUE(B33,B33+1)
27	=ACTIVATE(B8)
28	=INPUT(B30,2,B2)
29	=IF(OR(D28="Y",D28="y"),GOTO(D4),MESSAGE(FALSE))
30	=RETURN()
31	
32	
33	
34	
35	
36	
37	

Figure 7.9 Check subroutine

Immediately, you must determine if a worksheet is available to enter the check data. This is done by the IF command in D2, which checks the value contained in variable named *Chk*. If Chk contains the logical value FALSE, then no worksheet is available to enter check data. In this instance, the subroutine named *Check.Wks* is called to create another temporary worksheet.

If the variable Chk contains the logical value TRUE, a worksheet exists, and the MESSAGE command in D3 displays the message *Check Entry* immediately below the menu bar. This informs the user of the current operation. Then the worksheet, whose name appears in B8 of the macro sheet, is activated by the ACTIVATE command in D4. Named *Chk.Temp*, this is the temporary worksheet created by the Check.Wks subroutine.

The worksheet is prepared for data entry when the SELECT command in D4 selects cells B1 through B5 on the worksheet, and any information in the cells is deleted by the EDIT.DELETE command in D6. Notice that the value two is used to shift the cells up instead of to the right.

The worksheet is then formatted with the ALIGNMENT command in D7, which left justifies the cell data. This is followed by the SELECT command in D8, which selects B1 on the temporary worksheet in preparation for the first entry.

Once the worksheet is ready, data is entered by the routine that occupies cells D9 through D17 on the macro sheet. In sequence, the SELECT, FORMULA, and FORMAT.NUMBER commands occupying cells D9 through D17 select the correct cells on the temporary worksheet, obtain the data via the Input dialog box, enter it into the temporary worksheet, and format it correctly.

Notice the FORMULA command that appears in cell D18 of the macro sheet. It contains a minus sign immediately preceding the INPUT command. Since all checks will be entered as negative numbers, this little trick automatically converts the amount of theelcheck to a negative number before it's placed into the temporary worksheet.

The amount of the check is then formatted by the FORMAT. NUMBER command in D19. Cell B16 is selected, and the user is asked to verify that the information shown on the monitor is correct —performed by the INPUT command in D21.

If the user provides a negative response, the IF command in D22 branches to cell D5 and allows the information to be re-entered. If a positive response is given, the check data is transferred to the CR.Data worksheet.

Although the same method in the deposit routine for transferring data to the CR.Data worksheet could be used, there is an alternative method that requires only a single command. This reduces the number of commands required and entirely removes the need for a loop, but it is not suitable for all occasions. It involves the use of arrays, and therefore must be used with care.

Before the data can be transferred, the correct cells must be selected. The CR.Data worksheet is activated by the ACTIVATE command in D23, and the SELECT command in D24 uses two OFFSET commands to select the cell range extending from column A to column E. The row number is designated by the number of entries contained in cell B33 of the macro sheet.

Next, a variation of the FORMULA command, called FORMULA.ARRAY, enters an array formula consisting of the TRANSPOSE command into the currently active cell on the CR.Data worksheet. This transfers the data from cells B1 through B5, using RC-style addressing, to the cells in column A through column E.

Thus, the FORMULA.ARRAY command is used the same way the FORMULA command is. The only difference is that the FORMULA.ARRAY command simulates holding down the Command key when the formula is entered.

After the data is transferred, the value in B33 on the macro sheet is incremented by the SET.VALUE command in D26, to maintain the correct number of items on the CR.Data worksheet. The temporary worksheet used for entering checks is activated by the command in D27, and the user is asked if there is another entry to be made.

If the user responds with a positive reply (indicated by either an uppercase or lowercase "Y"), the GOTO command in D29 branches to D4. Otherwise, the message displayed below the menu bar disappears and the routine ends at the RETURN command in A30.

Check.Wks Subroutine

The subroutine that creates the temporary worksheet for entry of check data is named *Check.Wks*, and is located in cells D38 through D60 (Figure 7.10). Its commands and operation are virtually identical to the Deposit.Wks routine, except for the worksheet name it assigns to the temporary worksheet (Chk.Temp instead of Dep.Temp), the number of cells used in the worksheet (five instead of four), and the named variable used to indicate the presence or absence of the worksheet (Chk instead of Dep).

	D
38	*Check.Wks*
39	=NEW(1)
40	=SELECT(!A1)
41	=FORMULA("Check #: ")
42	=SELECT(!A2)
43	=FORMULA("Check Date: ")
44	=SELECT(!A3)
45	=FORMULA("Memoranda: ")
46	=SELECT(!A4)
47	=FORMULA("Category: ")
48	=SELECT(!A5)
49	=FORMULA("Amount: ")
50	=SELECT(!A1:A5)
51	=COLUMN.WIDTH(12)
52	=ALIGNMENT(4)
53	=STYLE(TRUE,FALSE)
54	=COLUMN.WIDTH(25,!B1)
55	=SELECT(!B1)
56	=SET.NAME("Chk",TRUE)
57	=DISPLAY(FALSE,FALSE,FALSE)
58	=FULL(TRUE)
59	=SAVE.AS(B8)
60	=RETURN()
61	

Figure 7.10 Check.Wks subroutine

Since it offers nothing new in the way of procedures, methods, or commands, you shouldn't have any trouble understanding its operation.

Printing the Check Register

Periodically you'll want to print a report that shows all the activity in your check register. The Register subroutine will not only prepare and print this report, it will also compute the current balance of your checking account.

When the user chooses selection number three of the menu, the IF command in A14 will call the subroutine named *Register*, which occupies cells E1 through E26 on the macro sheet (Figure 7.11).

Upon entry, the ACTIVATE command in E2 activates the CR.Data worksheet and selects columns A and B. The SELECT and ALIGN-MENT commands in E3 and E4 center the data.

Columns D and E are individually selected and formatted by the commands that appear in E5 through E8, which is followed by the selection and alignment of the titles that appear in cells A1 through E1 by the two commands in E9 and E10.

In E11 a new command, SELECT.LAST.CELL, is used to select the last cell on the CR.Data worksheet. Assuming that the worksheet has not been disturbed, this command will select the last cell in column E.

Next, the size of the worksheet is determined in preparation for computing the current balance. The compound command in E12 first determines the number of rows that are contained between cell A1 and the currently selected cell (which is the last cell on the worksheet). The formula

ROWS(!A1:SELECTION())

calculates the number of rows, and the macro adds two to this figure to allow for the balance. The final value is assigned the name *Size*, which will be used as the row offset value in the next command.

	E
1	*Register*
2	=ACTIVATE("CR.Data")
3	=SELECT(!A:B)
4	=ALIGNMENT(3)
5	=SELECT(!D:D)
6	=ALIGNMENT(3)
7	=SELECT(!E:E)
8	=ALIGNMENT(4)
9	=SELECT(!A1:E1)
10	=ALIGNMENT(3)
11	=SELECT.LAST.CELL()
12	=SET.NAME("Size",ROWS(!A1:SELECTION())+2)
13	=SELECT(OFFSET(!A1,Size,2))
14	=FORMULA("Current Balance")
15	=SELECT(OFFSET(!A1,Size,4))
16	=FORMULA("=SUM(C5:C5)")
17	=SELECT(!A1:SELECTION())
18	=SET.PRINT.AREA()
19	=PAGE.SETUP(E25,E26,1,1,1,1,FALSE,FALSE)
20	=PRINT?()
21	=DELETE.NAME("Size")
22	=RETURN()
23	
24	*Page Setup Data (Header and Footer)*
25	&LCheck Register Worksheet&R&D &T
26	&CPage &P
27	

Figure 7.11 Register subroutine

In E13, the SELECT command selects the cell that is *Size* number of rows down and two columns over from cell A1 on the CR.Data worksheet. If all has gone well, this will be the Memorandum column.

The FORMULA command in E14 then enters the words *Current Balance* into the active cell on the worksheet, leaving one blank row between the active cell and the data appearing above it on the worksheet.

In a similar manner, the commands in E15 and E16 select the corresponding cell that appears in the column labeled Amount in preparation for entering a formula that will compute the current balance of the check register.

The FORMULA command in E16 enters a formula using RC-style addressing within the SUM function into the currently active cell. This formula totals all positive and negative numbers in column five. This total figure is the current balance.

After the current balance has been computed, the macro prepares the worksheet for printing. The command in E17 selects all cells on the worksheet that contain data, and the SET.PRINT.AREA command in E18 establishes the printing area. The SET.PRINT.AREA command is equivalent to the SET.PRINT.AREA option of the Options menu.

Next, the PAGE.SETUP command uses the information displayed in cells E25 and E26 of the macro sheet as header and footer, specifies a left, right, top, and bottom margin setting of one inch, and prevents the *Print Row & Column Headings* and the *Print Gridlines* option boxes from containing an X. This provides a more appealing report format.

Once the print area and basic printing options have been established, the report header and footer are created. The data in E25 incorporates special characters, each preceded by the ampersand, to form the header that will left justify (*&L*) the words *Check Register*, and right justify the following: the current date (caused by the designation &D) followed by one space and the current time (caused by the designation &T).

The footer information in E26 uses the designation &C to center the word *Page*, which is followed by the designation &P, that will cause the current page number to be printed.

You should note that the PAGE.SETUP command can also be replaced with a variation that will allow the user to specify all of the data concerning the page setup by the following command.

$$= PAGE.SETUP?()$$

If used, this command will display the Page Setup window, letting the user establish all page options. It is the same as choosing Page Setup from the File menu.

In E20, the command PRINT?() is the equivalent of choosing the Print... option of the FORMULA menu. The PRINT?() command will allow the user to print the worksheet, preview the worksheet, or cancel the printing command. To prevent the user from having these choices, remove the question mark that appears in the command.

After the check register is printed, the DELETE.NAME command in E21 removes the named definition *Size*, and the subroutine ends with the RETURN command in E22.

Status

There are many times when you will not want to print the entire check register, just find out the current balance. When that time arrives, you need only choose selection number five of the menu; the subroutine named Status will quickly give you the status of your check register. (If you're wondering what happened to menu selection number four, due to its size and complexity it's discussed separately in Chapter 8.)

When the user chooses selection five of the menu, the IF command in A16 on the macro sheet calls the subroutine named *Status*, which begins in cell F1 (see Figure 7.12).

	F
1	*Status*
2	=ALERT(F7&F6,2)
3	=RETURN()
4	
5	*Computes Current Balance*
6	=TEXT(SUM(CR.Data!$E:$E),"$#,###.00 ;($#,###.00)")
7	Present Balance is:
8	
9	

Figure 7.12 Status subroutine

Since it isn't necessary to obtain any information from the user, a Note Alert dialog box will be used to display the information. The ALERT command in F2 on the macro sheet uses the cell references F7 and F6 as the source for the information that will be displayed in the dialog box. The number 2 that appears in the parentheses specifies that this will be a Note Alert and only an OK button will be displayed. The ampersand between the command joins the contents of the two cells so they will appear as one phrase.

In cell F7, the phrase "Present Balance is: " must have a space following the colon to provide a visually appealing display.

The entry for cell F6 consists of a compound command that uses an external reference to obtain and correctly format the current balance. First, the SUM function obtains the present balance of the entries found in column E of the CR.Data worksheet. Once this figure is obtained, the TEXT command, which converts numbers to text, converts the current balance to text in the format shown after the comma that follows the SUM function. Thus, this single command is equivalent to three different commands: SUM, FORMAT.NUMBER, and TEXT.

The dialog box will be displayed on the upper portion of the monitor and, after the user clicks OK, the RETURN command in F3 ends the subroutine, sending control back to cell A17.

By using a single dialog box and one compound command, you enable the user to obtain the current balance quickly at any time by making a single menu selection.

Quitting

When the user has finished with the check register, selection six of the menu causes the macro to end properly, leaving no open worksheets..

When the user chooses selection six of the menu, the IF command in A17 branches to cell A19. This calls a subroutine named *Clean.Up*, which occupies cells A52 through A69, as shown in Figure 7.13.

	A
52	*Clean.Up*
53	=IF(Dep=FALSE,GOTO(A57))
54	=ACTIVATE(B7)
55	=Save.It()
56	=FILE.DELETE(B7)
57	=IF(Chk=FALSE,GOTO(A61))
58	=ACTIVATE(B8)
59	=Save.It()
60	=FILE.DELETE(B8)
61	=IF(Rpt=FALSE,GOTO(A65))
62	=ACTIVATE(B9)
63	=Save.It()
64	=FILE.DELETE(B9)
65	=IF(Sum=FALSE,GOTO(A69))
66	=ACTIVATE(B10)
67	=Save.It()
68	=FILE.DELETE(B10)
69	=RETURN()
70	

Figure 7.13 Clean.Up subroutine

The Clean.Up routine simply checks to see if the temporary worksheet used to enter deposits is open. If Dep.Wks is open, Clean.Up activates it with the command in A54. The subroutine saves the worksheet on the disk (A55), then immediately deletes the file and closes the worksheet.

This procedure is performed for each of the temporary worksheets so that the user is left with a clean display. When all of the temporary worksheets have been closed, the subroutine returns and continues execution with the command in A20.

After closing all worksheets, the subroutine resets all variables. In A20, the *Init.Vars* subroutine is again called to set to false all variable names that indicate the presence of temporary worksheets.

Next, the commands in A21 through A23 activate the CR.Data worksheet, save it to the disk, then close it. Activating, saving, and closing CR.Data makes sure that all transactions entered have been recorded and agree with the number of items maintained in cell B33 of the macro sheet.

The CR.Menu is then activated and closed by the commands in cells A24 and 25. This worksheet doesn't have to be saved since there were no entries actually made on it.

Finally, the CR.Macro sheet is activated by the command in A26, then saved by the **SAVE** command in A27 so that the figure shown in B33 is correctly maintained. The entire macro is ended with the **RETURN** command in A28.

Summary

In this chapter you learned how to create worksheets that can be used as menus and process the user's selection. You saw how one controlling routine can access several subroutines that perform a variety of functions, from displaying a single Alert box to compiling and printing a report.

You examined different methods for transferring information from one worksheet to another, by using the clipboard or transposing an array.

In the next chapter, you'll expand on these procedures to create a sophisticated report that automatically categorizes and summarizes worksheet data.

CHAPTER

Summary Report

In this chapter you'll create a macro that will automatically compile a report using the data in the CR.Data worksheet. This macro will summarize all deposits and expenditures by category, sort the report by category, and compute subtotals for each category — without knowing how many categories you are using or what they are.

The Summary subroutine incorporates some of the most sophisticated routines available through Excel's macros and demonstrates their power. If you understand the concepts, methods, and procedures presented in this chapter, you'll be able to create macros that dazzle the mind.

Occupying cells G37 through I37, the Summary subroutine is nothing more than a loop that controls seven individual subroutines. The success of many of the functions performed by some of the subroutines is entirely dependent on the position of the active cell. Be sure to note the position of the active cell each time a worksheet is activated or deactivated. This method alone will greatly increase the speed of your macros.

Before each routine is examined individually, a general description of what happens in each subroutine will familiarize you with the operation of each. This general description will be followed by an examination of the individual subroutines in the sequence they will be called.

139

When the user chooses selection number four of the menu, the Summary subroutine (shown in Figure 8.1) is activated and immediately calls Subroutine1 to create and format a new worksheet. The worksheet is saved with the name that appears in cell B10 on the macro sheet.

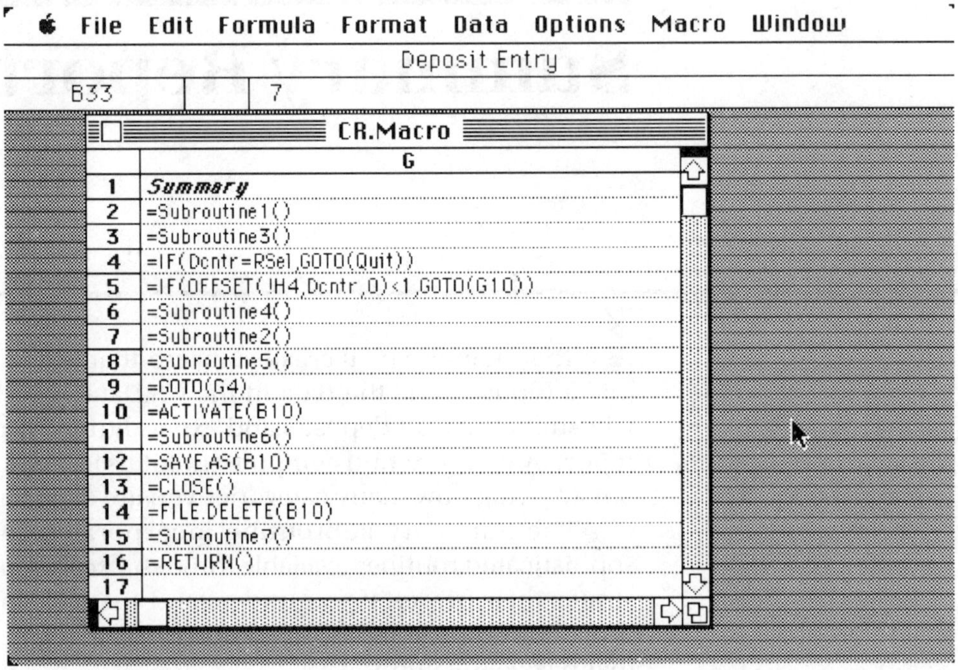

Figure 8.1 Summary subroutine to compile a report automatically

After the worksheet is created and formatted, Subroutine3 is called to establish a database area and to sort the data on the CR.Worksheet. Subroutine3 also extracts the contents of certain cells which will be used as criteria for extracting other data on the CR.Worksheet, in preparation for summarizing the data on the report.

Next, a loop repetitively calls Subroutine4, Subroutine2, and Subroutine5. Subroutine4 selects one item from a list and uses it to establish criteria. All records that meet the criteria specified are extracted.

Subroutine2 then copies the current cell selection to the clipboard and activates the worksheet named *Sum.Temp*. The data on the clipboard is pasted into the currently selected cells on the Sum.Temp worksheet, completing the transfer of one category from the CR.Data worksheet to the Sum.Temp worksheet.

Subroutine5 positions the active cell, enters an identification phrase into a cell below the data pasted into the Sum.Temp worksheet, and enters a formula into the adjacent cell. This formula provides a subtotal for the category.

Upon completion of the loop, Subroutine6 establishes the final totals for the worksheet, formats the worksheet, establishes the page setup parameters, and prints the report shown in Figure 9.1, p. 163.

After the report has been printed, the Sum.Temp worksheet is saved and deleted, and Subroutine7 is called to remove all temporary data (such as the criteria areas) from the CR.Data worksheet.

Subroutine1

The first subroutine that is called by the Summary subroutine is located in cells G18 through G30. It is named Subroutine1 and is shown in Figure 8.2.

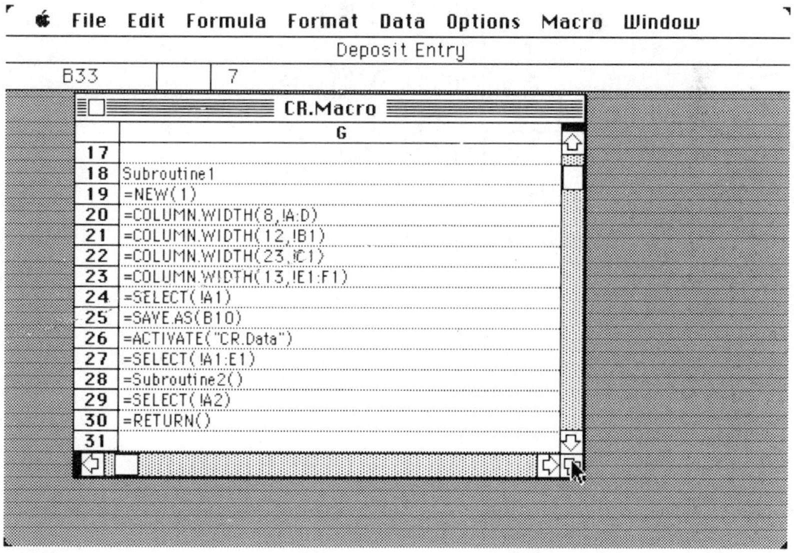

Figure 8.2 Subroutine1 to open Sum.Temp worksheet but not select the cells

Subroutine1 first opens a new worksheet (G19) and sets the widths of columns A through F without using the SELECT command to actually select the cells. Setting column width without selecting cells is accomplished by the variation of the COLUMN.WIDTH command shown in cells G20 through G23.

The SELECT command in G24 makes cell A1 the active cell, and the command in G25 saves the worksheet with the name Sum.Temp.

Next, the CR.Data worksheet is activated, the SELECT command in G27 selects cells A1 through F1, and Subroutine2 is called. After Subroutine2 completes its function, the SELECT command in G29 selects cell A2 on the CR.Worksheet, and Subroutine1 is ended by the RETURN command in G30.

Subroutine2

The second subroutine, named Subroutine2 and shown in Figure 8.3, is called by many routines. This subroutine works regardless of the actual status of both worksheets. Its purpose is to copy the contents of the active cell selection to the Sum.Temp worksheet.

	G
32	Subroutine2
33	=COPY()
34	=ACTIVATE(B10)
35	=PASTE()
36	=RETURN()
37	

Figure 8.3 Subroutine2 to transfer one category to Sum.Temp worksheet

Before Subroutine2 is called, a certain range of cells on one worksheet (usually the CR.Data worksheet) has been selected, and at least one cell on another worksheet (usually Sum.Temp) has been selected. Subroutine2 copies the data from the first range of cells to the clipboard with the COPY command in G33, activates the Sum.Temp worksheet (G34), and pastes the information into the active cell with the paste command in G35. The RETURN command in G36 ends the macro.

This subroutine takes advantage of one of Excel's little-noted features: it automatically expands the cell range where data will be pasted to match the size of the cell range that was copied. As such, you need be concerned only with the location of the first cell when pasting material and don't have to worry about determining the correct size of the paste range.

Subroutine3

After Subroutine2 has completed its operation, the command in cell G3 calls Subroutine3. Subroutine 3 (Figure 8.4) determines the size of the CR.Data worksheet, sorts the worksheet, and extracts one category of data.

	H
1	Subroutine3
2	=ACTIVATE("CR.Data")
3	=SET.NAME("First",!A1)
4	=SELECT.LAST.CELL()
5	=SET.NAME("NRows",ROWS(!A1:SELECTION()))
6	=SET.NAME("Last",OFFSET(!E1,Rows,0))
7	=SELECT(First:Last)
8	=SET.DATABASE()
9	=SORT(1,!$D$2,1)
10	=SELECT(!D1)
11	=COPY()
12	=SELECT(!G1)
13	=PASTE()
14	=SELECT(!G3)
15	=PASTE()
16	=SELECT(!G2)
17	=CLEAR(3)
18	=SELECT(!G1:G2)
19	=SET.CRITERIA()
20	=SELECT(!G3:OFFSET(!G3,NRows,0))
21	=EXTRACT(TRUE)
22	=SET.NAME("RSel",ROWS(SELECTION()))
23	=SELECT(!H4:OFFSET(!H4,RSel-1,0))
24	=FORMULA.FILL("=LEN(RC[-1])")
25	=SET.NAME("Dcntr",0)
26	=SELECT(!A1:E1)
27	=COPY()
28	=SELECT(!I1:M1)
29	=PASTE()
30	=RETURN()
31	
32	Subroutine7
33	=ACTIVATE("CR.Data")
34	=SELECT(!$F:$M)
35	=EDIT.DELETE(1)+SELECT(!A1)
36	=SAVE()
37	=RETURN()

Figure 8.4 Subroutine3 to establish a database and sort data

As soon as the macro begins execution, the command in H2 activates the CR.Data worksheet, and the SET.NAME command in H3 assigns the name *First* to cell A1 on the CR.Data worksheet.

Next, the SELECT.LAST.CELL command selects the last active cell on the worksheet in preparation for determining the size of the worksheet.

In H5, the SET.NAME command defines the name *NRows* as the total number of rows containing data on the worksheet. It is important that you do not insert or delete any information on the CR.Data worksheet, since doing so may invalidate this calculation.

After the number of rows has been determined, the value contained in NRows is used as the row offset figure by the command in H6 to assign the name *Last* as the last active cell in column E. H7 then selects all cells from First to Last, which includes all transactions entered in the CR.Data worksheet.

With the entire active area of the worksheet selected, the SET.DATABASE command in H8 defines the active area as a database area, which is then sorted by categories.

The SORT command in H9 is equivalent to choosing the Sort option of the Data menu, specifying a sort by row (indicated by the first "1") using the information in cell D2 as the sort key, and sorting in ascending order (indicated by the second "1").

After the worksheet has been sorted, a criteria area is created on the CR.Data worksheet. The SELECT command in H10 selects the entry in cell D1, then the COPY command in H11 copies the data to the clipboard. This is the column heading (or field label), which is used to establish a criteria area when H12 selects cell G1 on the CR.Data worksheet and H13 pastes the contents of the clipboard into the cell.

The commands in cells H14 and H15 on the macro sheet then select cell G3 on the worksheet and again paste the column heading into it. The data pasted into cell G3 are used for the Data Extract, which will be performed momentarily.

The SELECT and CLEAR commands in H16 and H17 select cell G2 — where the criteria will normally be found — and clear all formulas, formats, and so on, by specifying the third option of the command. This ensures that only the data specified by cell G3 will be extracted and is equivalent to choosing the Clear option of the Edit menu.

Once the cell has been cleared, the command in H18 selects cells G1 and G2 on the CR.Data worksheet. These cells are defined as the criteria area by the SET.CRITERIA command in H19. At this time, the active area of the worksheet has been established as a database area, and a criteria area has been set up in cells G1 and G2.

The OFFSET command in H20 selects a cell range from G3 down, extending as many rows as are contained in the database. This ensures enough cells will be selected to accommodate all category definitions that exist in column D of the worksheet. If enough cells were not selected, it is possible that some categories on the CR.Data worksheet would be omitted from the report.

After selecting the cells, the EXTRACT command uses the TRUE option to extract all category definitions found in column D but excludes any duplicates. This leaves a clean list of categories, which appear in sorted order, that can be used to compile a summary report. You should note that after the extraction is performed, the number of cells selected is reduced.

The total number of categories is determined by the SET.NAME command in H22. This command determines the number of rows contained in the current selection, then stores the value in the named definition RSel. With just a slight modification, this figure provides the total number of categories contained in the CR.Data worksheet.

Next, the total length of each category is determined. The SELECT and OFFSET commands in H23 are combined to select a cell range that is equivalent in size to the data extracted, beginning with cell H4 on the macro sheet. The FORMULA.FILL command in H24 enters the formula

$$=LEN(RC[-1])$$

into each cell. This provides the length of the entry in the corresponding cells of column G. Thus, as soon as a length of zero is encountered, one can safely assume that the end of the list has been reached.

In H25, a temporary counter named *Dcntr* is created with an initial value of zero. It keeps track of which category in the list beginning at cell G4 will be used as the current criteria element.

Finally, the commands in H26 through H29 select all of the labels appearing in cells A1 through E1 on the CR.Data worksheet, copy them, then paste them into cells I1 through M1 to be used for extracting information from the database. And naturally, the subroutine ends at the RETURN command in H30.

The comparison in G4 of the Summary subroutine is a safety valve that compares *Dcntr* to *Rsel*, the number of rows in the criteria extraction area, to see if their values are equal. If they ever are equal —which shouldn't happen — control automatically branches to the RETURN command in G16 to immediately terminate processing.

Cell G5 begins a loop that will call three subroutines (Subroutine4, Subroutine2, and Subroutine5) as long as the length in cell H4 plus the offset of *Dcntr* (the current criteria item) is *not* less than one. When Dcntr is less than one, the last criteria item has been processed and the loop is ended with a branch to cell G10.

Subroutine4

The purpose of Subroutine4 is to choose one of the category items in column G, insert it into the criteria area (cells G1 and G2), select the extraction range, and extract all records that meet the criteria. *Notice that the extracted records remain selected when the subroutine ends*.

When the command in G6calls Subroutine4 (Figure 8.5) , execution begins with the SELECT command in I2. This command uses the value currently contained in *Dcntr* to select the cell in column G that contains the first criteria item.

	I
1	Subroutine4
2	=SELECT(OFFSET(!G4,Dcntr,0))
3	=COPY()
4	=SELECT(!G2)
5	=PASTE()
6	=SELECT(!I1:OFFSET(!I1,NRows,4))
7	=EXTRACT(TRUE)
8	=SET.NAME("Trows",ROWS(SELECTION())-1)
9	=SELECT(!I2:OFFSET(!I2,Trows,5))
10	=RETURN()
11	

Figure 8.5 Subroutine4 to select an item for establishing criteria

You can create the criteria for the current category by copying the contents of the active cell to the clipboard by the COPY command in I3. Next, cell G2 on the CR.Data worksheet is selected (I4), and the data is pasted into the criteria area with the PASTE command in I5.

Next, the SELECT and OFFSET commands are combined in I6 to select a range of cells, extending from columns I1 through M1, which is NRows in length. The EXTRACT command in I7 extracts all records that meet the current criteria.

The number of rows contained in the extracted selection is determined and saved in the named reference *Trows* by the SET.NAME command in I9, and Subroutine 4 ends with the RETURN in I10.

Upon return from Subroutine4, cell G7 of the Summary routine immediately calls Subroutine2. If you remember, the purpose of Subroutine2 is to copy the currently selected cell range, activate the Sum.Temp worksheet, and paste the information into the worksheet beginning with the currently selected cell. This is the reason that it's important to leave the active cell on the Sum.Temp worksheet in column A, ready for the next pasting. Otherwise, the wrong data may be transferred.

Subroutine5

When Subroutine2 has finished, cell G8 of the Summary routine calls Subroutine5 to insert a formula in the correct cell to provide a subtotal for the current category.

Subroutine5 occupies cells I12 through I21 and is shown in Figure 8.6.

	I
12	Subroutine5
13	=SELECT(OFFSET(SELECTION(),Trows,0))
14	=SELECT("RC[+2]")
15	=FORMULA("Subtotal This Category")+STYLE(FALSE,TRUE)
16	=SELECT("RC[+3]")
17	=FORMULA("=SUM(R[-1]C[-1]:R[-"&Trows&"]C[-1])")+STYLE(FALSE,TRUE)
18	=SELECT("R[+1]C[-5]")
19	=SET.NAME("Dcntr",Dcntr+1)
20	=ACTIVATE("CR.Data")
21	=RETURN()
22	

Figure 8.6 Subroutine5 to subtotal the current category

When Subroutine5 begins execution, Sum.Temp is still the active worksheet and has had information pasted into it, but the *position* of the active cell *has not been changed.* So if the active cell was initially A2 and five rows of data were pasted in by Subroutine 2, the selected cell range would extend from A2 through E6, and A2 would be the active cell in the selection.

The correct location for the subtotal information is determined by the SELECT command in I13. This command first moves the position of the active cell to one row below the information that was pasted into the worksheet, which would be A7 (assuming that five rows were pasted in). This SELECT command also ensures that only one cell is now selected.

Next, the SELECT command again positions the active cell two rows to the right, using the relative option of RC addressing. This is the Memorandum column.

Take a close look at the entry in cell I15 on the macro sheet. The FORMULA command, which enters the phrase "Subtotal This Category," is followed by the STYLE command to display the data in italics. By separating the two commands with a plus symbol, you instruct Excel to enter the phrase "Subtotal This Category," and display it in italics.

Formally, this is known as *concatenation* of commands. The *Excel User's Guide* makes a point of stating that there are no advantages to be derived from concatenation and that it makes reading the program more difficult. You will find, however, that sometimes a macro you want to print is just a hair too long to fit on one page. Instead of having to print an entire second page that contains only two or three commands, you can use concatenation to make the macro short enough to fit on one page.

Further, since Excel defines the active area of a worksheet by rectangles, making a macro shorter may help you gain a small savings in memory usage.

To select the correct cell for the subtotal formula, RC addressing is used again in cell I16 with the SELECT command to position the active cell *one column to the right* of the Amount column. This will enable the subtotals for each category to stand out from the rest of the material in the worksheet.

Once the position of the active cell is determined, a seemingly complex command is used in I17 to total all amounts for the current category, then display the total in italics.

The first address within the SUM function specifies the cell that is one row above and one column to the left of the currently selected cell. Next, Trows — which contains the number of rows in the selection that were pasted into the worksheet by Subroutine2 — determines the position of the first row within the category.

Since it's a named definition, the portion of the formula that reads

R[-"&Trows&"]

simply uses the defined value of Trows as a number. Without the ampersands and quotation marks, the command, which would read R[-Trows], would produce an error message when Excel attempted to execute it, since Trows is not a number *when it's enclosed in quotation marks*.

The correct column, one to the left, is then specified by the second C[-1] that appears in the command. Thus, the results of the formula are to determine the starting and ending cells to be used by the SUM command.

And again, the STYLE command is concatenated so that the contents will be displayed in italics.

The SELECT command in I18 then positions the active cell in column A (five rows to the left of the current cell) and one row down from the current cell.

In I19, the SET.NAME command increments the value of *Dcntr* in preparation for the next category; the ACTIVATE command activates the CR.Data worksheet in preparation for the next pass through the loop; and the RETURN in I21 ends the subroutine.

After Subroutine5 is completed, the GOTO command in G9 of the Summary subroutine sends execution back to cell G4 for another pass through the loop. The Summary subroutine will continue to loop until all categories have been processed, at which time the macro resumes execution with the ACTIVATE command in G10, which will activate the Sum.Temp worksheet.

At this time, the category data has been transferred, and the subtotals have been entered and displayed in italics.

Subroutine6

After all of the categories have been transferred to the Sum.Temp worksheet (which must be active), Subroutine6 (Figure 8.7) is called by the command in G11 to prepare the worksheet for printing.

	I
23	Subroutine6
24	=SELECT("R[+2]C[+2]")
25	=FORMULA("Total All Categories")+STYLE(TRUE,FALSE)
26	=SELECT("RC[+3]")
27	=FORMULA("=SUM(R[-3]C:R2C)")+STYLE(TRUE,FALSE)
28	=SELECT(!$E:$F)
29	=FORMAT.NUMBER("$#,###.00 ;($#,###.00)")
30	=SELECT(!$B:$B)
31	=FORMAT.NUMBER("MMM. D, YYYY")
32	=ALIGNMENT(3)
33	=SELECT(!$D:$D)
34	=ALIGNMENT(3)
35	=PAGE.SETUP("&LSummary Report&R&D","&CPage &P",0.5,0.5,1,1,FALSE,FALSE)
36	=PRINT?()
37	=RETURN()
38	

Figure 8.7 Subroutine6 to prepare the worksheet for printing

When Subroutine6 begins execution, the SELECT command in I24 moves the active cell down two rows and to the right two columns (again into the Memorandum column). The FORMULA command in I25 enters the phrase that will be used to identify the grand total, and the STYLE command displays it in bold italics.

Next, the cell three columns to the right of the current cell is selected (I26), and the formula to total all of the subtotal figures is entered by the formula in I27.

Columns E and F are selected, and the figures contained in those columns are formatted by the commands in I28 and I29, while the commands in I30 through I34 format the remaining data on the worksheet.

In cell I35, the PAGE.SETUP command establishes the header, footer, left and right margins of .5 inch each and top and bottom margins of one inch each, and it sets rows/column headings and gridlines to false.

At this point, the worksheet is properly formatted and ready to be printed, and the PRINT command in I36 is used to give the user control over the number of copies to be printed.

After the printing operation has been performed, the subroutine ends with the RETURN in I37.

Finally, the Sum.Temp worksheet is saved with the SAVE.AS command in G12, and closed by the command in G13. Then the Sum.Temp worksheet is deleted with the FILE.DELETE command in G14.

Subroutine7

The final subroutine shown in Figure 8.8, Subroutine7, is then called to perform a bit of cleanup on the CR.Data worksheet.

	H
32	Subroutine7
33	=ACTIVATE("CR.Data")
34	=SELECT(!$F:$M)
35	=EDIT.DELETE(1)+SELECT(!A1)
36	=SAVE()
37	=RETURN()
38	

Figure 8.8 Subroutine7 to clean up the CR.DAta worksheet

The purpose of Subroutine7 is simply to remove all material that was added by the Summary subroutine. This is accomplished by activating the worksheet (H33), selecting columns F through M (H34), deleting the columns with the EDIT.DELETE command in H35, and then selecting A1 on the CR.Data worksheet before saving the worksheet with the SAVE command in H36.

The RETURN command in H37 returns execution to cell G16, which ends the entire Summary subroutine with the RETURN command in that cell.

Final Touch

Since it's relatively easy to make typographical errors when entering a macro from a book, and even harder to test and debug it with the macro spread over an entire chapter, Figure 8.9 contains a complete listing of the entire macro.

	A	B
1	*Menu*	*General Data*
2	=MESSAGE(TRUE,B4)	Verify Data
3	=Init.Var3()	Is the information shown correct (Y=Yes, N=No)?
4	=Open.Wks()	Initializing All Functions. Please Wait.
5	=MESSAGE(TRUE,B13)	*Temporary Worksheet File Names*
6	=ACTIVATE("CR.Menu")	Dep.Temp.
7	=INPUT(B14,7,B13)	Chk.Temp.
8	=IF(A7=FALSE,GOTO(A28))	Rpt.Temp.
9	=SET.VALUE(A7,VALUE(A7))	Sum.Temp.
10	=IF(OR(A7<1,A7>6),Error1(),GOTO(A12))	*Menu Data*
11	=GOTO(A7)	Transaction Selection
12	=IF(A7=1,Deposit())	Enter your selection by number
13	=IF(A7=2,Check())	Your selection must be a number between 1 and 6.
14	=IF(A7=3,Register())	
15	=IF(A7=4,Summary())	*Deposit Data*
16	=IF(A7=5,Status())	Enter date of deposit (Example: MM/DD/YY).
17	=IF(A7=6,GOTO(A19))	Enter memoranda for deposit
18	=GOTO(A5)	Enter category of deposit
19	=Clean.Up()	Enter deposit amount (No $ symbol , No commas).
20	=Init.Var3()	Enter another deposit (Y=Yes, N=No)?
21	=ACTIVATE("CR.Data")	*Check Data*
22	=SAVE()	Enter check number
23	=CLOSE()	Enter date of check (Example: MM/DD/YY)
24	=ACTIVATE("CR.Menu")	Enter memoranda for check
25	=CLOSE()	Enter category of check
26	=ACTIVATE("CR.Macro")	Enter check amount (No $ symbol , No commas)
27	=SAVE()	Enter another check (Y=Yes, N=No)?
28	=RETURN()	
29		*Number of entries on CR.Data Worksheet*
30	*Error1*	0
31	=ALERT(B15,3)	
32	=RETURN()	
33		
34		
35		
36		
37		

Figure 8.9 CR.Macro listing

	A	B
38	*Init.Vars*	
39	=SET.NAME("Dep.",FALSE)	
40	=SET.NAME("Chk.",FALSE)	
41	=SET.NAME("Rpt.",FALSE)	
42	=SET.NAME("Sum",FALSE)	
43	=RETURN()	
44		
45	*Open.Wks*	
46	=OPEN("CR.Data")	
47	=FULL(TRUE)	
48	=OPEN("CR.Menu")	
49	=FULL(TRUE)	
50	=RETURN()	
51		
52	*Clean.Up*	
53	=IF(Dep=FALSE,GOTO(A57))	
54	=ACTIVATE(B7)	
55	=Save.It()	
56	=FILE.DELETE(B7)	
57	=IF(Chk=FALSE,GOTO(A61))	
58	=ACTIVATE(B8)	
59	=Save.It()	
60	=FILE.DELETE(B8)	
61	=IF(Rpt=FALSE,GOTO(A65))	
62	=ACTIVATE(B9)	
63	=Save.It()	
64	=FILE.DELETE(B9)	
65	=IF(Sum=FALSE,GOTO(A69))	
66	=ACTIVATE(B10)	
67	=Save.It()	
68	=FILE.DELETE(B10)	
69	=RETURN()	

Figure 8.9 CR.Macro listing (continued)

	C *Deposit*	D *Check*
1	Deposit	Check
2	=IF(Dep=FALSE,Deposit.Wks())	=IF(Chk=FALSE,Check.Wks())
3	=MESSAGE(TRUE,"Deposit Entry.")	=MESSAGE(TRUE,"Check Entry.")
4	=ACTIVATE(B7)	=ACTIVATE(B8)
5	=SELECT(!B1:B4)	=SELECT(!B1:B5)
6	=EDIT.DELETE(2)	=EDIT.DELETE(2)
7	=ALIGNMENT(2)	=ALIGNMENT(2)
8	=SELECT(!B1)	=SELECT(!B1)
9	=FORMULA(INPUT(B18,1,B17))	=FORMULA(INPUT(B25,2,B24))
10	=FORMAT.NUMBER("mmmm d, yyyy")	=SELECT(!B2)
11	=SELECT(!B2)	=FORMULA(INPUT(B26,1,B24))
12	=FORMULA(INPUT(B19,2,B17))	=FORMAT.NUMBER("mmmm d, yyyy")
13	=SELECT(!B3)	=SELECT(!B3)
14	=FORMULA(INPUT(B20,2,B17))	=FORMULA(INPUT(B27,2,B24))
15	=SELECT(!B4)	=SELECT(!B4)
16	=FORMULA(INPUT(B21,1,B17))	=FORMULA(INPUT(B28,2,B24))
17	=FORMAT.NUMBER("$#,##0.00")	=SELECT(!B5)
18	=SELECT(!B16)	=FORMULA(-INPUT(B29,1,B24))
19	=INPUT(B3,2,B2)	=FORMAT.NUMBER("$#,##0.00;($#,##0.00)")
20	=IF(OR(C19="N",C19="n"),GOTO(C5))	=SELECT(!B16)
21	=SET.NAME("Dcntr",0)	=INPUT(B3,2,B2)
22	=ACTIVATE(B7)	=IF(OR(D21="N",D21="n"),GOTO(D5))
23	=SELECT(OFFSET(!B1,Dcntr,0)	=ACTIVATE("CR.Data")
24	=COPY()	=SELECT(OFFSET(!A2,B33,0),OFFSET(!A2,B33,4))
25	=ACTIVATE("CR.Data")	=FORMULA.ARRAY("=TRANSPOSE(Chk.Temp!R1C2:R5C2)")
26	=SELECT(OFFSET(!B2,B33,Dcntr))	=SET.VALUE(B33,B33+1)
27	=PASTE()	=ACTIVATE(B8)
28	=IF(Dcntr<3,SET.NAME("Dcntr",Dcntr+1),GOTO(C30))	=INPUT(B30,2,B2)
29	=GOTO(C22)	=IF(OR(D28="Y",D28="y"),GOTO(D4),MESSAGE(FALSE))
30	=SET.VALUE(B33,B33+1)	=RETURN()
31	=ACTIVATE(B7)	
32	=INPUT(B22,2,B2)	
33	=IF(OR(C32="Y",C32="y"),GOTO(C4),MESSAGE(FALSE))	
34	=RETURN()	
35		
36		
37		

Figure 8.9 CR.Macro listing (continued)

	C	D
38	*Deposit.Wks*	*Check.Wks*
39	=NEW(1)	=NEW(1)
40	=SELECT(IA1)	=SELECT(IA1)
41	=FORMULA("Deposit Date: ")	=FORMULA("Check #: ")
42	=SELECT(IA2)	=SELECT(IA2)
43	=FORMULA("Memoranda: ")	=FORMULA("Check Date: ")
44	=SELECT(IA3)	=SELECT(IA3)
45	=FORMULA("Category: ")	=FORMULA("Memoranda: ")
46	=SELECT(IA4)	=SELECT(IA4)
47	=FORMULA("Amount: ")	=FORMULA("Category: ")
48	=SELECT(IA1:A4)	=SELECT(IA5)
49	=COLUMN.WIDTH(12)	=FORMULA("Amount: ")
50	=ALIGNMENT(4)	=SELECT(IA1:A5)
51	=STYLE(TRUE,FALSE)	=COLUMN.WIDTH(12)
52	=COLUMN.WIDTH(25,IB1)	=ALIGNMENT(4)
53	=SELECT(IB1)	=STYLE(TRUE,FALSE)
54	=SET.NAME("Dep.",TRUE)	=COLUMN.WIDTH(25,IB1)
55	=DISPLAY(FALSE,FALSE,FALSE)	=SELECT(IB1)
56	=FULL(TRUE)	=SET.NAME("Chk",TRUE)
57	=SAVE.AS(B7)	=DISPLAY(FALSE,FALSE,FALSE)
58	=RETURN()	=FULL(TRUE)
59		=SAVE.AS(B8)
60		=RETURN()
61		
62		
63		
64		
65		
66		
67		
68		
69		

Figure 8.9 CR.Macro listing (continued)

	E	F
1	*Register*	*Status*
2	=ACTIVATE("CR.Data")	=ALERT(F7&F6,2)
3	=SELECT(!A:B)	=RETURN()
4	=ALIGNMENT(3)	*Computes Current Balance*
5	=SELECT(!D:D)	=TEXT(SUM(CR.Data!$E:$E),"$#,###.00_);($#,###.00)")
6	=ALIGNMENT(3)	Present Balance is:
7	=SELECT(!E:E)	
8	=ALIGNMENT(4)	
9	=SELECT(!A1:E1)	
10	=ALIGNMENT(3)	
11	=SELECT.LAST.CELL()	
12	=SET.NAME("Size",ROWS(!A1:SELECTION())+2)	
13	=SELECT(OFFSET(!A1,Size,2))	
14	=FORMULA("Current Balance")	
15	=SELECT(OFFSET(!A1,Size,4))	
16	=FORMULA("=SUM(C5:C5)")	
17	=SELECT(!A1:SELECTION())	
18	=SET.PRINT.AREA()	
19	=PAGE.SETUP(E25,E26,1,1,1,FALSE,FALSE)	
20	=PRINT?()	
21	=DELETE.NAME("Size")	
22	=RETURN()	
23		
24	*Page Setup Data (Header and Footer)*	
25	&LCheck Register Worksheet&R&D &T	
26	&CPage &P	
27		
28		
29		
30		
31		
32		
33		
34		
35		
36		
37		

Figure 8.9 CR.Macro listing (continued)

	G	H
1	*Summary*	Subroutine3
2	=Subroutine1()	=ACTIVATE("CR.Data")
3	=Subroutine3()	=SET.NAME("First",!A1)
4	=IF(Dcntr=RSel,GOTO(Quit))	=SELECT.LAST.CELL()
5	=IF(OFFSET(!H4,Dcntr,0)<1,GOTO(G10))	=SET.NAME("NRows",ROWS(!A1:SELECTION()))
6	=Subroutine4()	=SET.NAME("Last",OFFSET(!E1,Rows,0))
7	=Subroutine2()	=SELECT(First:Last)
8	=Subroutine5()	=SET.DATABASE()
9	=GOTO(G4)	=SORT(1,!D$2,1)
10	=ACTIVATE(B10)	=SELECT(ID1)
11	=Subroutine6()	=COPY()
12	=SAVE.AS(B10)	=SELECT(IG1)
13	=CLOSE()	=PASTE()
14	=FILE.DELETE(B10)	=SELECT(IG3)
15	=Subroutine7()	=PASTE()
16	=RETURN()	=SELECT(IG2)
17		=CLEAR(3)
18	Subroutine1	=SELECT(IG1:G2)
19	=NEW(1)	=SET.CRITERIA()
20	=COLUMN.WIDTH(8,!A:D)	=SELECT(IG3,OFFSET(IG3,NRows,0))
21	=COLUMN.WIDTH(12,!B1)	=EXTRACT(TRUE)
22	=COLUMN.WIDTH(23,!C1)	=SET.NAME("RSel",ROWS(SELECTION()))
23	=COLUMN.WIDTH(13,!E1:F1)	=SELECT(IH4,OFFSET(IH4,RSel-1,0))
24	=SELECT(!A1)	=FORMULA.FILL("=LEN(RC[-1])")
25	=SAVE.AS(B10)	=SET.NAME("Dcntr",0)
26	=ACTIVATE("CR.Data")	=SELECT(!A1:E1)
27	=SELECT(!A1:E1)	=COPY()
28	=Subroutine2()	=SELECT(!I1:M1)
29	=SELECT(!A2)	=PASTE()
30	=RETURN()	=RETURN()
31		
32	Subroutine2	Subroutine7
33	=COPY()	=ACTIVATE("CR.Data")
34	=ACTIVATE(B10)	=SELECT(I$F:$M)
35	=PASTE()	=EDIT.DELETE(1)+SELECT(!A1)
36	=RETURN()	=SAVE()
37		=RETURN()

Figure 8.9 CR.Macro listing (continued)

1	Subroutine4
2	=SELECT(OFFSET(IG4,Dcntr,0))
3	=COPY()
4	=SELECT(IG2)
5	=PASTE()
6	=SELECT(II1:OFFSET(II1,NRows,4))
7	=EXTRACT(TRUE)
8	=SET.NAME("Trows",ROWS(SELECTION())-1)
9	=SELECT(II2:OFFSET(II2,Trows,5))
10	=RETURN()
11	
12	Subroutine5
13	=SELECT(OFFSET(SELECTION(),Trows,0))
14	=SELECT("RC[+2]")
15	=FORMULA("Subtotal This Category")+STYLE(FALSE,TRUE)
16	=SELECT("RC[+3]")
17	=FORMULA("=SUM(R[-1]C[-1]:R[-&Trows&"]C[-1])")+STYLE(FALSE,TRUE)
18	=SELECT("R[+1]C[-5]")
19	=SET.NAME("Dcntr",Dcntr+1)
20	=ACTIVATE("CR.Data")
21	=RETURN()
22	
23	Subroutine6
24	=SELECT("R[+2]C[+2]")
25	=FORMULA("Total All Categories")+STYLE(TRUE,FALSE)
26	=SELECT("RC[+3]")
27	=FORMULA("=SUM(R[-3]C:R2C)")+STYLE(TRUE,FALSE)
28	=SELECT(I$E:$F)
29	=FORMAT.NUMBER("$#,##0.00 ;($#,##0.00)")
30	=SELECT(I$B:$B)
31	=FORMAT.NUMBER("MMM D, YYYY")
32	=ALIGNMENT(3)
33	=SELECT(I$D:$D)
34	=ALIGNMENT(3)
35	=PAGE.SETUP("&LSummary Report&R&D","&CPage &P",0.5,0.5,1,1,FALSE,FALSE)
36	=PRINT?()
37	=RETURN()

Figure 8.9 CR.Macro listing (continued)

Before you use this macro, make sure that names have been assigned to all subroutines and that you assign the name *Start* to cell A1. You may also find it helpful to insert temporarily the STEP command into cell A1, so you can follow each command as it executes.

When you're reasonably sure (is anyone ever positive?) that all is in order, enter some phoney data into the CR.Worksheet and then choose selection number four of the menu. Your final results should resemble the sample report shown in Figure 8.10.

Summary Report					1/5/87
Check #	**Date**	**Memoranda**	**Category**	**Amount**	
	Oct. 27, 1986	Daily Sales Receipts	DS	$1,234.56	
	Oct. 29, 1986	Daily Sales Receipts	DS	$987.21	
		Subtotal This Category			*$2,221.77*
1003	Oct. 29, 1986	Computer Disk Sales	EQ	$55.00	
		Subtotal This Category			*$55.00*
1002	Oct. 28, 1986	Coffee Makers of America	MS	$12.23	
1005	Oct. 19, 1986	Coffee 'N Donuts To Go	MS	$6.89	
		Subtotal This Category			*$19.12*
1001	Oct. 28, 1986	Office Supply Company	OS	$24.56	
1004	Oct. 29, 1986	Office Supply Company	OS	$43.67	
		Subtotal This Category			*$68.23*
		Total All Categories			**$2,364.12**

Figure 8.10 Sample summary report made by CR.Macro

Summary

In this chapter you examined some of Excel's less frequently used capabilities to compile and categorize worksheet data and to transfer information between worksheets.

You learned how to use subroutines that are totally independent from the operation of all other subroutines (see Subroutine2), you learned how to concatenate commands and streamline your macros.

CHAPTER

Forms Design

Certainly one of Excel's least exploited capabilities is its ability to design reports that look like reports, invoices that look like invoices, and even personalized form letters. Even though you can't match the flexibility of dedicated software for generating forms, you can create forms that are visually appealing.

This chapter examines the five elements required for producing forms: page setup, column width, font size, alignment, and print area. Add to this Excel's advanced string manipulation capabilities and a touch of creativity, and you can produce everything from dynamic reports to personalized form letters.

Types

Multicolumn forms are generally used to create invoices, purchase orders, and other types of business forms that require the data to be in a column format, while single-column forms are better suited to such non-columnar formats as form letters and interoffice correspondence.

To design a multicolumn form such as an invoice, open a new worksheet and access the Page Setup option of the File menu. The options available through this function create the general size and appearance of the form.

The first step in designing a multicolumn form is to determine the width of each line on your form. You determine line width by subtracting the total of the left and right margins from the total width of your paper in inches. For example, establishing a left and right margin of one inch when using a paper size of 8.5 by 11 inches will leave 6.5 inches available for data on each line.

Next, make certain that the headers and footers contain no information, that the Print Row & Column Headings and Print Gridlines option boxes are not checked, and that the top and bottom margins are set to one inch. This removes all row/column headings and gridlines, making your form appear as if it were specifically designed as a form.

After establishing the page setup parameters, you'll see that a dashed line now appears between columns E and F, as well as between rows 49 and 50 on your worksheet. This dashed line indicates the page boundaries.

To create the heading, select C1 through C3, enter the information shown below, then use the Alignment and Style options of the Format menu to center the data and display it in bold type.

Cell	Entry
C1	The Super Sales Company
C2	One Industrial Lane
C3	New York, NY 10001
C4	(212) 555-1212

Next, cells A12 through A14 contain the address of the company (or person) receiving the invoice. You can enter this information in one of two ways. First, you can simply type in the data, placing the company name in A12, the street address in A13, and the city, state, and zip code in A14.

Second, you can use external references to enter and format the address information automatically. For example, if you had a worksheet named *Clients* that contained the names and addresses of your clients (perhaps in columns A, B, and C), you might want to use the following.

Cell	Formula
A12	= "To: "&INDEX(CLIENTS!$A:$A,F1,0)
A13	= " "&INDEX(CLIENTS!$A:$A,F1,1)
A14	= " "&INDEX(CLIENTS!$A:$A,F1,2)

Then, any time you enter a number into cell F1 on the worksheet containing the invoice, Excel will automatically link the data from the Clients worksheet to the Invoice worksheet. And since cell F1 on the Invoice worksheet will be outside the print area, you need not worry about it being printed.

Next, the body of the invoice is created. For the date and invoice number, enter the words Date: and Invoice#: into D12 and D13; then use the Right option of the Alignment menu.

Next, select cells A18 through E18, choose the Bold option of the Style menu, and then enter the information shown below.

A18	Your Order
B18	Salesman
C18	Ship Via
D18	Terms
E18	FOB

In a similar manner, select cells A21 through E21, choose the Bold option of the Style menu to display the cell contents in bold type, then choose the Center option of the Alignment information and enter the information shown below.

A21	Stock No.
B21	Quantity
C21	Description
D21	Price Ea.
E21	Total

The final five entries required on the invoice are entered into cells D41 through D44 and also in C49 — the last available cell. The information in D41 is Total:, D42 is Shipping:, D43 is Tax:, and D44 is Amt. Due:. These entries are displayed in normal type and are left aligned.

The entry for C49, the phrase "No Returns Without Authorization," is centered and displayed in bold. Notice that when the Bold option is chosen, the phrase will extend slightly beyond the cell boundaries. This spillover is possible only if the adjoining cells are blank.

Next, select the cell range extending from A21 through E40, choose the Border option of the format menu, then check the Left, Right, Top, and Bottom options. If you check only the Outline option, Excel will outline the selection as a whole, not each individual cell.

Finally, set the area that will be printed by choosing cells A1 through E49 and then by accessing the Set Print Area option of the Options menu. When your form is printed, it should resemble the one shown in Figure 9.1.

The Super Sales Company
One Industrial Lane
New York, NY 10001
(212) 555-1212

Abington Distributors Inc.
875 West 39th Street
New York, NY 10002

Date: 9/21/86
Invoice #: A10734

Your Order	**Salesman**	**Ship Via**		**Terms**	**FOB**
PO 123456	Johnson	United Parcel Service		Net 30	Destination

Stock No.	Quantity	Description	Price Ea.	Total
			Total:	
			Shipping:	
			Tax:	
			Amt. Due:	

No Returns Without Authorization

Figure 9.1 Sample invoice designed as multicolumn form

The key to designing multicolumn forms is to organize your information carefully, then take advantage of Excel's formatting options to provide the appearance of a "regular" form. If you need a few ideas for forms, browse through any forms supply catalog.

If you find you need more or less space on your form, changing the font and point size can make quite a bit of difference.

Single Column Forms

The other major type of form is called a single-column form. Single-column forms are useful for reports, memos, and other documents that normally do not require the row/column format of invoices, purchase orders, and so on.

Again, open a new worksheet, immediately access the Page Setup menu, and set each of the options shown below as follows.

Header	None
Footer	None
Left Margin	1 inch
Right Margin	1 inch
Top Margin	0 inches
Bottom Margin	1 inch
Row/Column Headings	Not Checked
Gridlines	Not Checked

Next, select cell A1 and set the Column Width option of the Format menu to 65, which will allow only column A to be printed on your report.

Now you have a single, continuous page that can be used in much the same way a typewriter can: each cell corresponds directly to one printed line. All you need to do is enter the information you need anywhere on the form, using the various formatting options available (Bold, Italic, Center, etc.) to display certain parts of your document as you need them.

Since any data extending beyond the limits of the cell will not be printed, what you see when you set up a page this way is what you get. If some of your data extends beyond the limits of the cell, use Excel's editing features to cut and paste information to and from the Clipboard.

Even external references are easy to incorporate into your document, either by entering the reference in a cell by itself or by making use of the ampersand function. For example, the entry shown below would combine the contents of cell A2 on the Names worksheet with the word "Dear" to form a salutation.

= "Dear "&NAMES!$A$2

When you've finished writing your document, all you need do is simply select all cells containing data, choose the Set Print Option of the Options menu, then print your document.

Text Manipulation

Another useful feature of Excel is its ability to generate personalized form letters. Although this is normally considered to be a word processing application, with a little knowledge, a custom form, and a bit of creativity, you'll be able to send price lists, advertising, reports, or memos almost as fast as if you were using a word processor.

If you understand how to perform basic text manipulation (which is normally called *string manipulation*), you can write a macro that will automatically search your document for the occurrence of specific characters, then replace them with a different series of characters.

Open a new worksheet and enter the information shown in Figure 9.2.

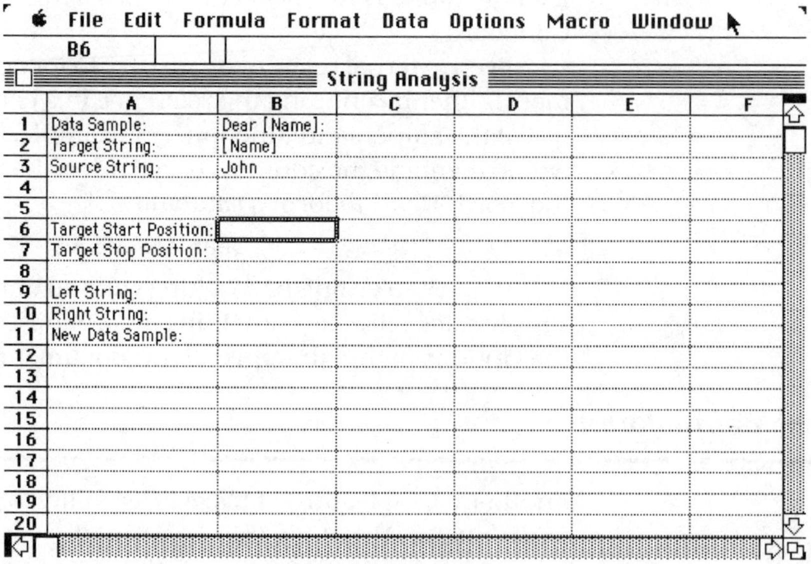

Figure 9.2 String Analysis worksheet

The information entered in column A will be used to identify the text and numbers displayed in the corresponding cells of column B. The first, located in B1, is a typical sample you might find in a form letter. You'll notice it includes what is sometimes called a *data specifier* (the item [Name]). This indicates where the data is to be inserted.

In B2, the data specifier (here called the *target string*) has been entered, as it will be used to help you understand how to manipulate text. The final item in B3 is called the *source string*, which is the information that will eventually replace the target string in the data specifier.

The first step to take in manipulating text is to identify the starting position within the data specifier of the target string. To find the starting position, use Excel's SEARCH command, which requires three parameters: the item you're searching for, which is the target string; the item to search, which is the data specifier; and the character position where the search is to begin.

Entering the formula

= SEARCH(B2,B1,1)

into cell B6 will cause the entry currently in B1 (the data specifier) to be searched for the entry currently in B2 (the target string), starting at the first character. This will cause the number six to be displayed in B6. If you count the characters in B1, you'll see that the entry in B2 (the target string) begins at the sixth character position.

Next, the ending position of the target string must be determined before it's possible to extract the target string from the data specifier. This is accomplished by entering the formula shown below into cell B7.

= B6 + LEN(B2)-1

This formula adds the starting position to the total length of the target string, then subtracts one, leaving a value of eleven — the position of the last character of the target string.

Once these two items have been determined, you only have to dissect the data specifier into two parts, left and right, inserting the source string between them, then recomposing the string.

To extract the left string, the MID function is used, which also requires three parameters: the text from which the data is to be extracted, the position where the extraction will start, and the number of characters to extract.

Select cell B9 and enter

= MID(B1,1,B6-1)

which will cause the first six characters — the starting position of the target string minus one — of cell B1 to be extracted and displayed in B6, as shown in Figure 9.3.

```
 ú  File  Edit  Formula  Format  Data  Options  Macro  Window
    B9              =MID(B1,1,B6-1)
```

	A	B	C	D	E	F
1	Data Sample:	Dear [Name]:				
2	Target String:	[Name]				
3	Source String:	John				
4						
5						
6	Target Start Position:	6				
7	Target Stop Position:	11				
8						
9	Left String:	Dear				
10	Right String:					
11	New Data Sample:					
12						
13						
14						
15						
16						
17						
18						
19						
20						

Figure 9.3 Left string extracted

In a similar manner, the MID function extracts the right string by using the stop position plus one as the starting point and the length of the data specifier minus the stop position as the number of characters to be extracted.

Selecting cell B10 on the String Analysis worksheet and entering the formula

$$= MID(B1,B7 + 1,LEN(B1)-B7)$$

will cause the colon to appear in cell B10, as shown in Figure 9.4.

File Edit Formula Format Data Options Macro Window

| B10 | =MID(B1,B7+1,LEN(B1)-B7) |

String Analysis

	A	B	C	D	E	F
1	Data Sample:	Dear [Name]:				
2	Target String:	[Name]				
3	Source String:	John				
4						
5						
6	Target Start Position:	6				
7	Target Stop Position:	11				
8						
9	Left String:	Dear				
10	Right String:	:				
11	New Data Sample:					
12						
13						
14						
15						
16						
17						
18						
19						
20						

Figure 9.4 Right string extracted

Once you've extracted the left and right strings (regardless of the fact that the right string used here is only one character in length), all you need do is concatenate the three elements to form a new string. Selecting cell B11 and entering the formula

= B9&B3&B10

will provide you with the new string shown in Figure 9.5.

 File   Edit   Formula   Format   Data   Options   Macro   Window

| B11 | | =B9&B3&B10 |

String Analysis

	A	B	C	D	E	F
1	Data Sample:	Dear [Name]:				
2	Target String:	[Name]				
3	Source String:	John				
4						
5						
6	Target Start Position:	6				
7	Target Stop Position:	11				
8						
9	Left String:	Dear				
10	Right String:	:				
11	New Data Sample:	Dear John:				
12						
13						
14						
15						
16						
17						
18						
19						
20						

Figure 9.5 Newly constructed string

Summary

These text manipulation techniques can be combined with the single-column forms design to address your invoices and purchase orders automatically, or to simulate an inexpensive word processor for distributing your worksheet information in the form of personalized reports and memos.

If you use the knowledge you've gained about macros, working with multiple worksheets, and Excel's integration capabilities, you can create macros that ask the user for specific information, create a worksheet to solve a particular problem, then distribute the results. All it takes is a bit of planning, a little work, and a dash of creativity.

Macro and Worksheet Library

The Case Function Macro

The Case macro sheet contains three function macros, named *Upper*, *Lower*, and *Words*. These macros are designed to manipulate the contents of text cells, providing you with the ability to convert the data in any cell to uppercase or lowercase, or to capitalize only the first letter of each entry. They can be used with text constants, cell references, or they can be called by other macros.

All of the macros are used in the same way, and they are all accessed by using the Paste Function Menu. After assigning the appropriate name (UPPER, LOWER, WORDS) to each of the macros via the Define Name option of the formula menu, you simply paste the appropriate function into a cell, click the OK button, and view the results.

The following examples show both the various types of entries using the macros and their results. Many of the examples include non-alphabetical characters like numbers, exclamation marks, and so on, to show that those characters are not affected by the macros.

You Enter:	The Results Are:
= UPPER("Hello")	HELLO
= UPPER("I'm 18 today!")	I'M 18 TODAY!
= LOWER("HeLlO")	hello
= LOWER("I'm 35 TODAY!")	i'm 35 today!
= WORDS("How much is it?")	How Much Is It?
= WORDS("Retail price is $35.00")	Retail Price Is $35.00
= UPPER(B1)	Text in cell B1 is converted to uppercase.
= LOWER(F3)	Text in cell F3 is converted to lowercase.
= WORDS($D$2)	Text in cell D2 has first letter of each word capitalized.

Macro Descriptions

All of the macros are similar in construction and use virtually the same commands. Understand how one operates, and you'll understand them all. The following line-by-line descriptions will explain what each command does. Just be sure to define the cells containing the names *UPPER*, *LOWER*, and *WORDS* as function macros by using the Define Name option of the Formula menu.

The Upper() Macro

The command in cell A2 of Figure A.1 defines the name *Txt* as either the cell reference or the text you enter when you paste the function into a cell on your worksheet. Next, the contents of the active cell on your worksheet are placed into cell D4 on the macro sheet by the SET.VALUE command in A3.

The SET.VALUE command is used again in cell A4 to establish the length of the text by using the Length function, the resulting value is placed into cell D5 on the macro sheet, and cell D6 is designated as a general purpose counter by another SET.VALUE command in cell A5.

	A
1	Upper
2	=ARGUMENT("Txt")
3	=SET.VALUE(D4,Txt)
4	=SET.VALUE(D5,LEN(Txt))
5	=SET.VALUE(D6,1)
6	=SEARCH(MID(D4,D6,1),D2,1)
7	=IF(ISERROR(A6),GOTO(A10))
8	=IF(D6=1,SET.VALUE(D7,MID(D3,A6,1)),SET.VALUE(D7,MID(D7,1,LEN(D7))&MID(D3,A6,1)))
9	=GOTO(A11)
10	=IF(D6=1,SET.VALUE(D7,MID(D4,D6,1)),SET.VALUE(D7,MID(D7,1,LEN(D7))&MID(D4,D6,1)))
11	=IF(D6=D5,GOTO(A13),SET.VALUE(D6,D6+1))
12	=GOTO(A6)
13	=RETURN(D7)
14	
15	

Figure A.1 UPPER Function Macro Listing

	D
1	Data Area
2	abcdefghijklmnopqrstuvwxyz
3	ABCDEFGHIJKLMNOPQRSTUVWXYZ
4	{Text passed by calling routine.}
5	{Length of text located in D4}
6	{Counter for primary loop}
7	{Converted text to be returned}
8	{Flag to indicate presence of a space}
9	
10	
11	
12	
13	
14	
15	

Figure A.2 Common Data Area

In cell A6, the MID function is combined with the SEARCH command to compare a single character of the text in cell D4 — the text to be converted — to the lowercase letters of the alphabet located in cell D2 on the macro sheet. So if the value in D6, which is the general purpose counter, is 2, the second letter of the text in D4 will be compared to each letter in D2 — the lowercase letters of the alphabet.

If the letter in D4 does not match any of the letters in D2, the SEARCH command will return an error value in cell A6 of the macro sheet, indicating that the search was not successful.

The ISERROR command in A7 checks the contents of A6 on the macro sheet to see if A6 contains an error value indicating that the character was not a lowercase letter. If an error condition exists ISERROR causes the macro to branch to cell A10.

The commands in A8 first check to see if the first character in the text is lowercase by seeing if the value in cell D6 on the macro sheet equals one. If so, then the uppercase equivalent of the character is extracted from cell D3 on the macro sheet by use of the MID function, which is placed into cell D7. If it isn't the first character (D6>1), then the uppercase equivalent of the last character checked is extracted from cell D3 and appended to the current contents of cell D7.

Next, the GOTO command in cell A9 is executed, which causes a branch to cell A11 to keep the command in cell A10 from being executed.

The command in A10 is executed only when an error value exists in cell A6, which only happens when the current character wasn't located during the search of the lowercase letters in D2. Its function is quite simple: append the current non-lowercase character to the entry in cell D7. This procedure ensures that all non-text characters and existing uppercase letters are included in the entry that will be returned.

The command in A11 compares the current value of the counter in D6 to the total length of the text entry in D5. If the two *are* equal, all characters have been processed and a branch is taken to cell A13, which will end the macro. If the two values *aren't* equal, there are more characters to be processed, and the counter value in D6 is incremented in preparation for the next character.

The command in A12 on the macro sheet then causes a branch back to A6 so that the next character in the text can be processed.

The RETURN command in A13 returns the value contained in D7 (the converted text) to the caller, usually a worksheet.

The LOWER() Macro

The macro named LOWER, listed in Figure A.3, occupies cells B1 through B13 and operates the same way the macro named UPPER does. The only difference in operation between the two macros is that the cell locations D2 and D3 are reversed.

By reversing the two cell designations, the macro reverses both the search and replacement functions, substituting the uppercase alphabet for the lowercase version and vice versa.

	B
1	Lower
2	=ARGUMENT("Txt")
3	=SET.VALUE(D4,Txt)
4	=SET.VALUE(D5,LEN(Txt))
5	=SET.VALUE(D6,1)
6	=SEARCH(MID(D4,D6,1),D3,1)
7	=IF(ISERROR(B6),GOTO(B10))
8	=IF(D6=1,SET.VALUE(D7,MID(D2,B6,1)),SET.VALUE(D7,MID(D7,1,LEN(D7))&MID(D2,B6,1)))
9	=GOTO(B11)
10	=IF(D6=1,SET.VALUE(D7,MID(D4,D6,1)),SET.VALUE(D7,MID(D7,1,LEN(D7))&MID(D4,D6,1)))
11	=IF(D6=D5,GOTO(B13),SET.VALUE(D6,D6+1))
12	=GOTO(B6)
13	=RETURN(D7)
14	
15	

Figure A.3 LOWER Function Macro Listing

The WORDS() Macro

The macro named WORDS occupies cells C1 through C14, listed in Figure A.4. With only a few differences, Words operates the same way the macros named UPPER and LOWER do.

The ARGUMENT command in C2 defines the text or cell reference on your macro sheet as the name *Txt*. The SET.VALUE command in C3 places the text to be converted into cell D5 on the macro sheet, while the SET.VALUE command in C4 establishes the total length of the text into cell D5.

The SET.VALUE commands in cells C5 and C6 on the macro sheet establish two general-purpose counters whose values are initially set to one. The SET.VALUE command in C7 ensures that there is no entry in cell D7 on the macro sheet. Cell D7 will contain the text to be returned after it has been converted.

The GOTO command in C8 causes a branch to cell C10 to prevent the command in C9 from being executed for the first character.

The command in C9 — which is not executed for the first character of the entry — checks the character preceding the current character (i.e., the current character minus one) to see if it is a space. If so, a flag in cell D8 is set to one; otherwise the flag in D8 is set to zero.

The SEARCH command in C10 works the same way its counterpart in cell A6 does, returning either an error value or the position of the character located.

The IF command in C11 is a modified version of the IF command in A8, incorporating the AND function to ensure that there is no error value in cell C10 and that the flag in D8 equals one. If both these conditions are true, then the current character is converted to uppercase.

In cell C12, the IF command simply compares the values of cells D5 and D6 on the macro sheet to see if all characters have been processed. If the values are equal, then the entire text conversion process has been completed, and a branch is taken to cell C14. Otherwise, the value in cell D6 is incremented and the GOTO command in C13 is executed. This causes Excel to branch back to cell C9 to process the next character.

Finally, the RETURN command in C14 ends the macro, returning the current contents of cell D7 on the macro sheet to the user.

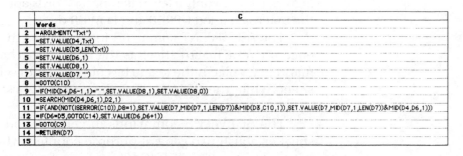

	c
1	Words
2	=ARGUMENT("Txt")
3	=SET.VALUE(D4,Txt)
4	=SET.VALUE(D5,LEN(Txt))
5	=SET.VALUE(D6,1)
6	=SET.VALUE(D8,1)
7	=SET.VALUE(D7,"")
8	=GOTO(C10)
9	=IF(MID(D4,D6-1,1)=" ",SET.VALUE(D8,1),SET.VALUE(D8,0))
10	=SEARCH(MID(D4,D6,1),D2,1)
11	=IF(AND(NOT(ISERROR(C10)),D8=1),SET.VALUE(D7,MID(D7,1,LEN(D7))&MID(D3,C10,1)),SET.VALUE(D7,MID(D7,1,LEN(D7))&MID(D4,D6,1)))
12	=IF(D6=D5,GOTO(C14),SET.VALUE(D6,D6+1))
13	=GOTO(C9)
14	=RETURN(D7)
15	

Figure A.4 WORDS Function Macro Listing

Alternative Uses and Modifications

Each of these macros can be called from another function macro by simply passing either the text to be converted or a cell reference. This is accomplished by using a command like = UPPER(*ref*) from within another macro. The *ref* can either be text enclosed with quotation marks or a cell reference.

By accessing the Define Name option of the Formula menu, you can change any of the macros from a function macro to a command macro, then include them as a subroutine in your other macros, or assign an "Option-Command-Key" to each.

File Manager Macro

Of all the macros you're likely to encounter, the File Manager macro must certainly rate among the shortest and most flexible. Consisting of only nine cells, it can be used as a subroutine within a command macro, converted to accept arguments like a function macro, or be used as an individual command macro.

To use it as a command macro that occupies cells A1 through A9 as shown in the listing below, simply place the name of the worksheet you need in cell B5 (on the macro sheet), and call the File Manager by using a command like = A1() or = File_Manager() (if you've named cell A1 File_Manager). If the worksheet is already open, File_Manager won't take any action. If the worksheet isn't open, File_Manager will open it. It's just that simple.

Cell	Command
A1	File_Manager
A2	= SET.NAME("Opn.Wks",DOCUMENTS())
A3	= SET.NAME("OpnCtr",COLUMNS(Opn.Wks))
A4	= SET.NAME("TCT",1)
A5	= IF(INDEX(Opn.Wks,TCT) = B5,RETURN())
A6	= IF(TCT = OpnCtr,GOTO(A8),SET.NAME("TCT",TCT + 1))
A7	= GOTO(A5)
A8	= OPEN(B5,TRUE)
A9	= RETURN()

Description

Cell A1 contains the name of the macro, which has been formally defined as a name by using the Define Name option of the Formula menu. When this routine is called, the SET.NAME command in cell A2 defines the name *Opn.Wks* as an array containing the names of all open documents.

In cell A3, the SET.NAME command is used again to establish the name *OpnCtr* as the number of open documents, and is followed by the SET.NAME in cell A4 which establishes the general-purpose counter named *TCT* and initializes its value to one.

Next, the INDEX command uses the current value of *TCT* to compare the name of an open document to the name of the worksheet in cell B5 of the macro sheet. If the two match, the worksheet name shown in B5 is already open, which causes the RETURN command in cell A9 to be executed, terminating the operation of File_Manager.

If the two worksheet names don't match, control passes to the IF command in A6, which compares the current value of *TCT* with the total number of open documents. If the two values are equal, all open worksheets have been checked, and control passes to the command in A8. Otherwise, *TCT* is incremented in preparation for checking the next worksheet name, and the GOTO command in A7 is executed.

In cell A8, the OPEN command is used to open the worksheet specified by the name in B5, and the TRUE option is used to open any linked documents.

Finally, the RETURN command in A9 is executed after the worksheet has been opened, returning control back to the caller.

Modifications

By inserting the argument command, = ARGUMENT("wks"), you can replace the reference to cell B5 that's in cell A5 with the argument being passed (*wks* in this example).

If you make the above modification and use the Define Name option of the Formula menu, you can (probably) convert File_Manager to a function macro, then use it in your worksheets or other macros without having to copy it.

Calendar Maker

The command macro shown in Figure A.5 lets you create an attractive calendar for any month between the years 1904 and 2040 by simply providing the starting date of the month.

To use the macro, choose the Run option of the Macro menu after opening the macro sheet, click Calendar_Maker!Start, then click the OK button. (You can also press Option-Command-c to start the macro, or change the lowercase letter c to any other key you desire by using the Define.Name option of the Formula menu and clicking the name *Start*.)

When the macro starts, you'll be asked to supply the starting date of the month in the form of MM/DD/YY (MM = Month; DD = Day; YY = Year). Simply enter a starting date like 6/1/86 (for June 1, 1986), click the OK button, and watch the macro do its thing!

You can include this macro in your own macros by changing the commands in cells A2 and A47. For example, if you define SD as the starting date before calling the macro, you can eliminate A2 entirely. You'll also probably want to change or eliminate the Save command in A47 so that your macro will maintain control over the worksheet.

Description

The SET.NAME command is combined with the INPUT command in cell A2 to establish the name SD as the starting date for the calendar, based upon the user's response to the input dialog box.

In A3, the NEW command opens a new worksheet and the display options formulas, gridlines, and heading are turned off by the DISPLAY command in A4.

Next, cells A3 through G3 on the worksheet are selected in A5 and the width for each column is set to nine by the COLUMN.WIDTH command in A6.

In A7, the BORDER command is used to outline each cell by specifying the left, right, top, and bottom borders as checked, and the outline option as unchecked. This method is used to ensure that each cell — instead of the entire range of cells — is outlined.

The general purpose counter named CTR is defined by the SET.NAME command in cell A8, and its initial value is set to zero.

	A	B
1	Make_Calendar Macro	Data Area
2	=SET.NAME("SD",INPUT(B2,2,B3))	Enter starting date (Example: 1/1/86 for January 1986)
3	=NEW(1)	Calendar Month Specification
4	=DISPLAY(FALSE,FALSE,FALSE)	Sunday
5	=SELECT(!A3:G3)	Monday
6	=COLUMN.WIDTH(9)	Tuesday
7	=BORDER(FALSE,TRUE,TRUE,TRUE,TRUE)	Wednesday
8	=SET.NAME("Ctr",0)	Thursday
9	=SELECT(OFFSET(!A3,0,CTR))	Friday
10	=FORMULA(OFFSET(B4,CTR,0))&ALIGNMENT(3)	Saturday
11	=IF(CTR=6,GOTO(A13),SET.NAME("CTR",CTR+1))	
12	=GOTO(A9)	
13	=SELECT(!A4:G21)	
14	=BORDER(,TRUE,TRUE,,)	
15	=SET.NAME("Ctr",0)	
16	=SELECT(OFFSET(!A6,CTR*3,0):OFFSET(!A6,CTR*3,6))	
17	=BORDER(,,,,TRUE)	
18	=IF(CTR=5,GOTO(A20),SET.NAME("Ctr",CTR+1))	
19	=GOTO(A16)	
20	=SELECT(!A1)	
21	=FORMULA(SD)&FORMAT.NUMBER("MMMM")	
22	=STYLE(TRUE,FALSE)&ALIGNMENT(2)	
23	=SELECT(!G1)	
24	=FORMULA(TEXT(SD,"YYYY"))	
25	=STYLE(TRUE,FALSE)&ALIGNMENT(4)	
26	=FULL(TRUE)	
27		
28	*This portion establishes the dates in the correct location.*	
29	=SET.NAME("WD",WEEKDAY(SD))	
30	=SET.NAME("CO",WD)	
31	=SET.NAME("RO",0)	
32	=SET.NAME("CD",1)	
33	=SELECT(OFFSET(!A4,RO,CO-1))	
34	=FORMULA(CD)	
35	=SET.NAME("CTR",MOD(CO,7))	
36	=SET.NAME("EM",!A1+CD)	
37	=IF(CTR=0,SET.NAME("RO",RO+3),GOTO(A39))	
38	=SET.NAME("CO",0)	
39	=SET.NAME("CO",CO+1)	
40	=SET.NAME("CD",CD+1)	
41	=IF(MONTH(!A1)=MONTH(EM),GOTO(A33))	
42	=SELECT(!A22)	
43	=FORMULA(" ")	
44	=HSCROLL(0%)	
45	=VSCROLL(0%)	
46	=PAGE.SETUP(" "," ",1.3,1,1,1,FALSE,FALSE)	
47	=SAVE.AS?()	
48	=RETURN()	
49		
50		
51		
52		

Figure A.5 Calendar_Maker Macro Listing

Cell A9 on the macro sheet is the beginning of a loop that will individually select a series of cells (A3 through G3), enter the days of the week, and format them correctly by using CTR as the row and column offset value. In A9, CTR is used as the column offset value to select the appropriate cell; while in A10 CTR is used as the row offset to choose the appropriate day of the week from cells B4 through B10 on the macro sheet, then enter it into the currently selected cell on the worksheet.

You'll notice two separate commands appear in A10, FORMULA and ALIGNMENT. This method is used here only as an aid in printing the macro listing, and does not increase the operational speed of the macro. It demonstrates that entering more than one command in a cell does not cause any adverse affects.

The IF command in A11 simply checks the current value of CTR to see if it equals six. If so, all seven days have been processed, and the macro branches to cell A13. Otherwise, the SET.NAME command increments the value contained in CTR, and the GOTO command in A12 causes a branch back to the beginning of the loop in A9 to process the next day of the week.

In cell A13, the SELECT command is used to select the cell range A4 through G21 — the active calendar area — and the BORDER command in cell A14 specifies the left and right options should be checked. Notice only two logical values are specified even though the BORDER command contains five options. By simply inserting the commas and ignoring the other options, you can change only the items you want without disturbing the other options.

In A15, the SET.NAME command is again used to set CTR to zero in preparation for completing the calendar display.

The SELECT command in A16 uses two offset commands to select a range of cells from column A through column G in increments of three cells. Thus, if CTR equals zero, cells A6 through G6 will be selected. If CTR equals one, cells A9 through G9 will be selected.

In A17 the variation of the BORDER command is used to underline each cell range selected by the command in A16, and the IF command in A18 compares the value of CTR to five. If CTR equals five, a branch is taken to cell A20, otherwise CTR is incremented and control of the macro branches back to cell A16 to process the next cell range.

The commands in cells A20, A21, and A22 simply select cell A1 on the worksheet, enter the starting date contained in the named reference SD, assign the numeric format "MMMM" (which causes the full name of the month to be displayed), display it in bold, and specify a left alignment.

The command in cells A23 through A25 perform a similar operation on cell G1, displaying the date as the full year (like 1986). The FULL command in A26 causes the worksheet to occupy the full screen area.

Cells A29 through A32 define four named references that will be used to establish the correct date in the proper weekday column. The names WD and CO contain the numeric representation of the day of the week, RO is set to one and will be used as the row offset, and CD is the column offset.

The commands in A33 and A34 simply select the appropriate cell and enter the date, and are followed by the SET.NAME command in A35. This time, CTR is set to equal the remainder of dividing the current day divided by seven, since there are seven days in a week.

In A36, the first day of the month is established in the named reference EM (short for "End of the Month"), which is used to determine if all the days in the month have been processed. Control of the macro proceeds to cell A37.

In A37, the column offset counter (CO) is checked for a value of zero. If CO equals zero, this is the first pass through the loop and it's necessary to increment the row offset counter and initialize the named references CO and CD. Otherwise, a branch is taken to A39.

The commands in A38, A39, and A40 simply establish the correct values for the column offset and current date, and the IF command in A41 checks the value of EM to see if it equals the current month. If so, the calendar is not complete and control passes back to A33 in preparation for handling the next date. Otherwise, the command in A42 is executed.

The SELECT command in A42 selects cell A22 on the worksheet and a space is entered by the FORMULA command in A43. This sets the active cell outside what will be the normal viewing area of the calendar so as not to detract from its appearance.

The HSCROLL and VSCROLL commands in A44 and A45 scroll the worksheet back to the beginning both horizontally and vertically, and the PAGE.SETUP command in A46 establishes the printing options required to print the calendar.

In A47, the Save.As? option of the save command is used to provide the user with the opportunity to save the worksheet; and the macro ends with the RETURN command in A48.

Additional Macros and Worksheets

You can obtain a complete list of macros and worksheets, including those listed throughout this book by sending your name and address to Richard Loggins, P.O. Box 39, Sugar Run, PA 18856.

Index